Life of Christ

Life of Christ

Illustrations by
Angus McBride

Hamlyn
London · New York · Sydney · Toronto

Published by
The Hamlyn Publishing Group Limited
London . New York . Sydney . Toronto
Astronaut House, Hounslow Road
Feltham, Middlesex
England

ISBN 0 600 31987 3

Filmset in the United Kingdom by Tradespools Ltd., Frome, Somerset, and by Headliners,
London.

Printed in Spain by Mateu Cromo, Madrid

The passage from Ernst Renan's *Life of Jesus* is reproduced by permission of
Pitman Publishing Limited, from the edition first published by C.A.Watts in 1935
in the Thinker's Library. The poem from 'Prayers on the Way of the Cross' by
Michel Quoist is reproduced from *Prayers of Life* by Michel Quoist, by kind
permission of Gill and Macmillan Limited. The extract from 'The Dream of
the Rood' is taken from *Anglo-Saxon Poetry, an essay with specimen translations*
by Gavin Bone, published by Oxford University Press, 1943, and is reprinted by permission
of the publisher. 'Mary Magdalen II' is reproduced from *Fifty Poems* by Boris Pasternak
published by George Allen and Unwin (Publishers) Limited, by kind permission of the
publisher. 'Journey of the Magi' is reproduced by permission of Faber and Faber Limited
from *Collected Poems 1909–1962* by T.S. Eliot.

The articles on 'The Political Background', 'Health and Healing', 'The Social Outcasts',
'The Law', 'The Dead Sea Scrolls and the Essenes', 'Women in Israel', 'The Messiah',
'The Temple', 'The Pharisees', 'The Zealots', 'The Sadducees' are written by
Margaret Offord.

The portrayal of Jesus has always been one of the greatest challenges presented to European artists, and the history of Western art was for a long time almost a record of their attempts to meet it. As the patronage of the Church gave way to that of the merchants, and more recently to that of industry, so did the artist's subject matter change, and today most 'biblical' illustration is treated only half-seriously as an element in children's books. Nowadays, children who are given any religious education are commonly confronted with pictorial images at best fashionable in style or gimmicky, and at worst sensationalistic or downright inaccurate. Adults, particularly in the Protestant denominations, are usually expected to take their religion without pictures, and their Bibles have no illustrations, And yet, all of us, old or young, in any part of the world, must rely greatly on imagination if we are to begin to understand the meaning of events that took place in Palestine nearly 2000 years ago, among vanished peoples and amid alien cultural surroundings.

Today we tend to want history rather than legend—archaeological truth rather than antiquarian theory—and inevitably, the period of Jesus' life has been subjected to the most intense critical scrutiny. Every historian (and any artist who attempts accurately to portray biblical events) is confounded by the dearth of visual information from this period. Whereas much more information exists than is generally realised, most of it conveys little idea of how things *looked*, and hardly anywhere is there a description of personal physical characteristics.

No one knows what Jesus, or any of his disciples or friends looked like. In spite of thousands of authoritative-sounding speculations over the years, we are still left with our individual imagination only—and that may be a good thing. Certainly, it leaves each of us, whether artists or not, free to picture Jesus as we wish—or as we need.

However, an illustration (if it is any good at all) will carry a certain conviction and should, at least, stimulate the imagination. With this in mind, I have planned these paintings so that they might work on more than one level. There are hints here and there—in the details, in the arrangement of the figures, in the lighting, even in the weather or time of day—of some of the unseen but none the less significant things that lay behind particular events.

In all these paintings I have tried to convey a facet of Jesus' extraordinary personality that I am convinced must have impressed his contemporaries as much as his teaching: his *energy*, the sheer power of his physical presence. There are no halos, no unearthly lights (except that which shines around the shepherds), only the lights and shades of the sun, moon, and stars—the lamps and fires of the natural world. Those were all that shone on Jesus when he lived on Earth. It was in men's hearts and souls that another kind of light came to surround his image and his name.

ANGUS MCBRIDE

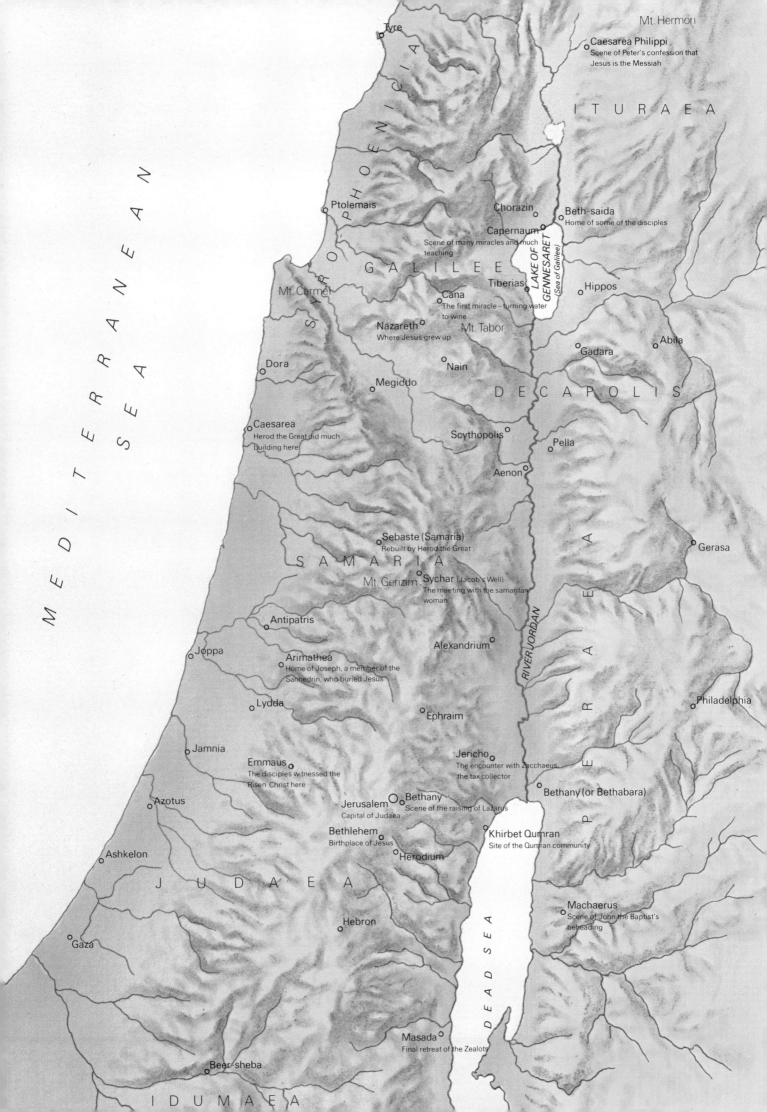

Mt. Hermon

ITURAEA

Caesarea Philippi
Scene of Peter's confession that
Jesus is the Messiah

Tyre

P
H
O
E
N
I
C
I
A

Ptolemais

Chorazin
Beth-saida
Home of some of the disciples

Capernaum
Scene of many miracles and much
teaching

GALILEE

LAKE OF
GENNESARET
(Sea of Galilee)

Mt. Carmel

Tiberias

Hippos

Cana
The first miracle – turning water
to wine

S
Y
R
O

Nazareth
Where Jesus grew up

Mt. Tabor

Dora

Nain

Gadara

Abila

Megiddo

DECAPOLIS

Caesarea
Herod the Great did much
building here

Scythopolis

Pella

Aenon

M
E
D
I
T
E
R
R
A
N
E
A
N

S
E
A

Sebaste (Samaria)
Rebuilt by Herod the Great

SAMARIA

Gerasa

Mt. Gerizim
Sychar (Jacob's Well)
The meeting with the samaritan
woman

Antipatris

Joppa

Alexandrium

P
E
R
A
E
A

Arimathea
Home of Joseph, a member of the
Sanhedrin, who buried Jesus

Philadelphia

Lydda

Ephraim

Jamnia

Emmaus
The disciples witnessed the
Risen Christ here

Jericho
The encounter with Zacchaeus,
the tax collector

Azotus

Bethany (or Bethabara)

Bethany
Scene of the raising of Lazarus

Jerusalem
Capital of Judaea

Bethlehem
Birthplace of Jesus

Khirbet Qumran
Site of the Qumran community

Ashkelon

Herodium

JUDAEA

Machaerus
Scene of John the Baptist's
beheading

Hebron

Gaza

D
E
A
D

S
E
A

Masada
Final retreat of the Zealots

Beer-sheba

R
I
V
E
R
J
O
R
D
A
N

IDUMAEA

St John
Chapter 1, verses 1-14

IN THE beginning was the Word, and the Word was with God, and the Word was God.

THE SAME was in the beginning with God.

ALL THINGS were made by him; and without him was not any thing made that was made.

IN HIM was life; and the life was the light of men.

AND THE light shineth in darkness; and the darkness comprehended it not.

THERE WAS a man sent from God, whose name was John.

THE SAME came for a witness, to bear witness of the Light, that all men through him might believe.

HE WAS not that Light, but was sent to bear witness of that Light.

THAT WAS the true Light, which lighteth every man that cometh into the world.

HE WAS in the world, and the world was made by him, and the world knew him not.

HE CAME unto his own, and his own received him not.

BUT AS many as received him, to them gave he power to become the sons of God, even to them that believe on his name:

WHICH WERE born, not of blood, nor of the will of the flesh, nor of the will of man, but of God.

AND THE Word was made flesh, and dwelt among us, (and we beheld his glory, the glory as of the only begotten of the Father,) full of grace and truth.

AND IN the sixth month the angel Gabriel was sent from God unto a city of Galilee, named Nazareth,

TO A virgin espoused to a man whose name was Joseph, of the house of David; and the virgin's name was Mary.

AND THE angel came in unto her, and said, Hail, thou that art highly favoured, the Lord is with thee: blessed art thou among women.

AND WHEN she saw him, she was troubled at his saying, and cast in her mind what manner of salutation this should be.

AND THE angel said unto her, Fear not, Mary: for thou hast found favour with God.

AND, BEHOLD, thou shalt conceive in thy womb, and bring forth a son, and shalt call his name JESUS.

HE SHALL be great, and shall be called the Son of the Highest: and the Lord God shall give unto him the throne of his father David:

AND HE shall reign over the house of Jacob for ever; and of his kingdom there shall be no end.

St Luke
Chapter 1, verses 46-55

AND MARY said, My soul doth magnify
the Lord,

AND MY spirit hath rejoiced in God
my Saviour.

FOR HE hath regarded the low estate of his
handmaiden: for, behold, from
henceforth all generations shall call
me blessed.

FOR HE that is mighty hath done to me
great things; and holy is his name.

AND HIS mercy is on them that fear him
from generation to generation.

HE HATH shewed strength with his arm;
he hath scattered the proud in the
imagination of their hearts.

HE HATH put down the mighty from their
seats, and exalted them of low degree.

HE HATH filled the hungry with good
things; and the rich he hath sent
empty away.

HE HATH holpen his servant Israel, in
remembrance of his mercy;

AS HE spake to our fathers, to Abraham,
and to his seed for ever.

AND SHE brought forth her first-born son, and wrapped him in swaddling clothes, and laid him in a manger; because there was no room for them in the inn.

AND THERE were in the same country shepherds abiding in the field, keeping watch over their flock by night.

AND, LO, the angel of the Lord came upon them, and the glory of the Lord shone round about them: and they were sore afraid.

AND THE angel said unto them, Fear not: for, behold, I bring you good tidings of great joy, which shall be to all people.

FOR UNTO you is born this day in the city of David a Saviour, which is Christ the Lord.

AND THIS shall be a sign unto you; Ye shall find the babe wrapped in swaddling clothes, lying in a manger.

AND SUDDENLY there was with the angel a multitude of the heavenly host praising God, and saying,

GLORY TO God in the highest, and on earth peace, good will toward men.

AND IT came to pass, as the angels were gone away from them into heaven, the shepherds said one to another, Let us now go even unto Bethlehem, and see this thing which is come to pass, which the Lord hath made known unto us.

AND THEY came with haste, and found Mary, and Joseph, and the babe lying in a manger.

St Matthew
Chapter 2, verses 1-12

NOW WHEN Jesus was born in Bethlehem of Judaea in the days of Herod the king, behold, there came wise men from the east to Jerusalem,

SAYING, Where is he that is born King of the Jews? For we have seen his star in the east, and are come to worship him.

WHEN HEROD the king had heard these things, he was troubled, and all Jerusalem with him.

AND WHEN he had gathered all the chief priests and scribes of the people together, he demanded of them where Christ should be born.

AND THEY said unto him, In Bethlehem of Judaea: for thus it is written by the prophet,

AND THOU Bethlehem, in the land of Juda, art not the least among the princes of Juda: for out of thee shall come a Governor, that shall rule my people Israel.

THEN HEROD, when he had privily called the wise men, enquired of them diligently what time the star appeared.

AND HE sent them to Bethlehem, and said, Go and search diligently for the young child; and when ye have found him, bring me word again, that I may come and worship him also.

WHEN THEY had heard the king, they departed; and, lo, the star, which they saw in the east, went before them, till it came and stood over where the young child was.

WHEN THEY saw the star, they rejoiced with exceeding great joy.

AND WHEN they were come into the house, they saw the young child with Mary his mother, and fell down, and worshipped him: and when they had opened their treasures, they presented him gifts; gold, and frankincense, and myrrh.

AND BEING warned of God in a dream that they should not return to Herod, they departed into their own country another way.

THE POLITICAL BACKGROUND (1)

The Jews believed that, as a result of God's covenant with Abraham, they were God's chosen people. They were aware of the need to preserve this special relationship by allowing God to permeate the whole of life, and consequently developed the idea of the theocratic state, where all law was submitted to the divine purpose. When Israel was independent, attempts could be made to put this idea into practice; when she was ruled by conquering powers, tension was the inevitable result.

For several hundred years before the birth of Christ, Israel was ruled by a succession of imperial powers: the Persians, the Seleucid Greeks, and finally the Romans. The Seleucids conquered Israel in 200 BC; they were at first tolerant overlords, giving freedom of religion and considerable political autonomy by delegating power to the High Priest. As a result of unrest and uprisings due to appalling social conditions, however, religious persecutions were started, which led to the revolt of the Maccabees (168–164 BC). This was successful in so far as it led to a truce, religious tolerance being granted in exchange for political obedience.

Meanwhile, the High Priests were gradually gaining more and more power until they ousted the Seleucids in 129 BC. Internal dissensions leading to civil war attracted a new power to the scene: Rome, with the general Pompey conquering Judaea in 63 BC. He began his rule badly by entering the sanctuary of the Temple – not an action which endeared him to his new subjects. He took all political power from the High Priest, thus weakening Judaea and making it a tributary of Rome. Caesar, who overthrew Pompey in 47 BC, was in some ways more lenient, giving back to the High Priest some of his old power. More significantly, he made the then adviser to the High Priest, Antipater the Idumaean, Governor of Judaea. It was the beginning of the Herodian dynasty.

The Idumaeans were prozelytes (gentile converts to Judaism)—a fact which was to arouse Jewish suspicion of them from the start—from south of Judaea; they were also political opportunists who, by ingratiating themselves with each of the Roman rulers in turn at a time when the dynasty of the High Priests was on the decline, managed to gain power. To strengthen his own position, Antipater gave important offices to his sons, one of whom began his career with an action which showed his pro-Roman sympathies and which displayed contempt for the supreme religious authorities: he executed a number of 'freedom fighters' without first consulting the Jewish Sanhedrin (court of law). He was to become Herod the Great.

Herod eventually ascended the throne of Judaea in 37 BC, through an act of typical political opportunism: he appealed to Rome during an uprising of the High Priestly dynasty, and predictably was granted an army large enough to capture Judaea. He presents historians with something of a paradox: how has this cruel and bloody monarch come to be known as 'great'? The greatness lies in his statesmanship and his political judgment, and his ability to come out on the winning side. Some see him as a realist: aware of the impossibility of Jewish independence, he sought for autonomy which would be gained by putting his country into a framework of order—which was how he saw the Roman Empire. To this end, he tried to encourage some cultural integration and was responsible for a vast programme of rebuilding in the Graeco-Roman style.

Whether Herod saw himself as guardian of the Jewish people in a pagan world, or whether he was just an opportunist tyrant, the result of his policies was the establishment of a police state. He not only condemned all those even remotely suspected of treason, including his own wife; he also instituted wholesale purges. His spies and secret police were everywhere; there are even apocryphal stories that he would walk in the streets in disguise, asking his subjects what they thought of him.

Towards the end of his life, Herod's persecution mania, and with it his atrocities, increased. Whatever its historical basis, it is not difficult to imagine the possibility of a 'Massacre of the Innocents' occurring around the time of the birth of Jesus. The advent of the mysterious Zoroastrian priests from the East asking the strange question 'Where is he who is born King of the Jews?' must have to Herod appeared as a terrible and frightening confirmation of the nagging doubts and fears that he, like many of his predecessors, might be overthrown. Yet where was this new suspect, this small baby who presented such a terrible threat? When the visitors had disappeared without trace, there could be no rest until all children under two, all possible suspects, were dead.

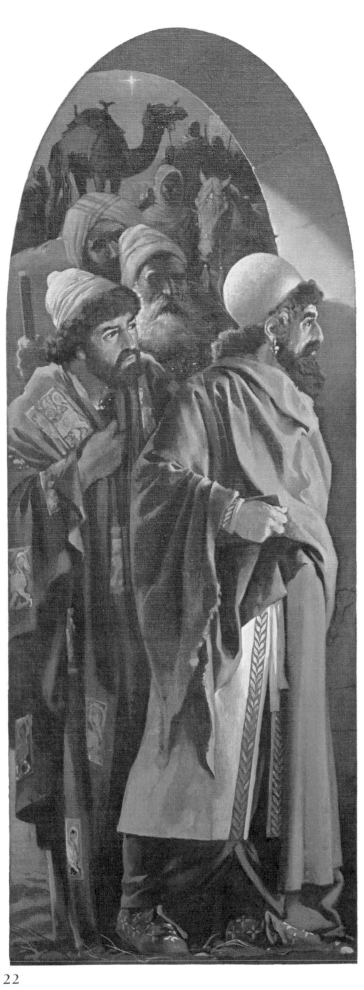
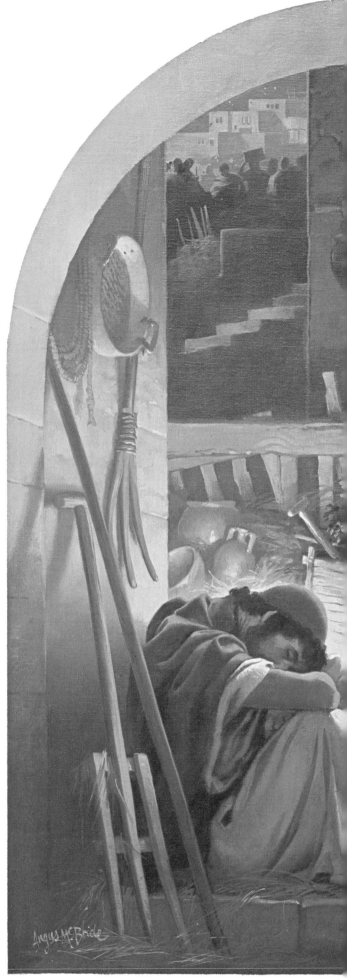

St Matthew
Chapter 2, verses 13-14

ND WHEN they were departed, behold,
the angel of the Lord appeareth to Joseph
in a dream, saying, Arise, and take the
young child and his mother, and flee into
Egypt, and be thou there until I bring thee
word: for Herod will seek the young child
to destroy him.

WHEN HE arose, he took the young child
and his mother by night, and departed
into Egypt.

THE POLITICAL BACKGROUND (2)

When Herod died in 4 AD, his kingdom was divided up between his three sons, Archelaus succeeding him in Judaea. Archelaus was a true son of his father and after one uprising ended with 3000 corpses in the Temple precinct, Judaea seemed close to revolution. Eventually, Archelaus was banished by the Romans, who instituted a form of direct rule in Judaea, with procurators from Rome. And so in AD 26 Pontius Pilate came on the scene. Pilate was a cruel man, who showed complete disregard for Jewish feelings. He executed patriots without trial, viciously put down any political resistance or manifestation of religious sentiment, and used Temple funds to build aqueducts. Eventually he too was recalled to Rome in AD 36.

The Herod referred to in the accounts of the ministry of Jesus is Herod Antipas, who ruled over Galilee. More sensible as a ruler than his father or his brother—although a notorious hedonist he was discreet enough to pay all respects due to the Temple—he is most famous for his clash with John the Baptist. Herod shared the fear of all his family for anything that might be regarded as subversive, and was thus suspicious of John and Jesus (who cuttingly referred to him as 'that fox'). Things came to a head when John spoke out against Herod's divorce and remarriage to his brother's widow, a thing forbidden by the Torah. John was imprisoned in the fortress of Machaerus. Herod's wife, greedy for revenge, engineered his end in a particularly spiteful way. At one of Herod's great parties, the king was so infatuated by his step-daughter Salome's dancing that he promised her anything she would ask for. Salome's reply, prompted by her mother, is well known: the Baptist's head on a plate.

Palestine at the time of Jesus was thus a political minefield. Any form of opposition to the regime was brutally suppressed by both the Romans and the Herods. In addition to the political terrors there was the burden of taxation, which was non-progressive and therefore very unjust, falling most heavily upon the poor. Taxes were collected by Jewish 'collaborators' (publicans). Particularly hated was the imperial census which involved registration at place of birth, and which must have more than anything brought home to the Jews the fact of their subjection to Rome. Although the Roman soldiers generally behaved with tact (the centurions in the Gospels emerge as courteous and circumspect), covering the image of the emperor on their shields when they marched through Judaea, the influence of a bad procurator could never-the-less turn the troops into merciless bullies.

A very early Christian tradition links Jesus' birth with an imperial census and with Bethlehem in Judaea. Whatever the historical truth of these accounts, their symbolic value is immense. God enters human history in the person of his Son at a time when his people are more than usually oppressed, in a place which is particularly ravaged by fear, brutality and man's inhumanity to man. What could better convey God's concern for the world, and his desire to identify with the sordid realities of the human condition?

The child Jesus in the Temple

St Luke

Chapter 2, verses 40-52

AND THE child grew, and waxed strong in spirit, filled with wisdom: and the grace of God was upon him.

NOW HIS parents went to Jerusalem every year at the feast of the passover.

AND WHEN he was twelve years old, they went up to Jerusalem after the custom of the feast.

AND WHEN they had fulfilled the days, as they returned, the child Jesus tarried behind in Jerusalem; and Joseph and his mother knew not of it.

BUT THEY, supposing him to have been in the company, went a day's journey; and they sought him among their kinsfolk and acquaintance.

AND WHEN they found him not, they turned back again to Jerusalem, seeking him.

AND IT came to pass, that after three days they found him in the temple, sitting in the midst of the doctors, both hearing them, and asking them questions.

AND ALL that heard him were astonished at his understanding and answers.

AND WHEN they saw him, they were amazed: and his mother said unto him, Son, why hast thou thus dealt with us? behold, thy father and I have sought thee sorrowing.

AND HE said unto them, How is it that ye sought me? wist ye not that I must be about my Father's business?

AND THEY understood not the saying which he spake unto them.

AND HE went down with them, and came to Nazareth, and was subject unto them: but his mother kept all these sayings in her heart.

AND JESUS increased in wisdom and stature, and in favour with God and man.

IN THOSE days came John the Baptist, preaching in the wilderness of Judaea,

AND SAYING, Repent ye: for the kingdom of heaven is at hand.

FOR THIS is he that was spoken of by the prophet Esaias, saying,
The voice of one crying in the wilderness, Prepare ye the
way of the Lord, make his paths straight.

AND THE same John had his raiment of camel's hair, and a
leathern girdle about his loins; and his meat was
locusts and wild honey.

THEN COMETH Jesus from Galilee to Jordon unto John, to be baptized of him.

BUT JOHN forbad him, saying, I have need to be baptized of thee, and comest thou to me?

AND JESUS answering said unto him, Suffer it to be so now: for thus it becometh us to fulfil all righteousness. Then he suffered him.

AND JESUS, when he was baptized, went up straightway out of the water: and, lo, the heavens were opened unto him, and he saw the Spirit of God descending like a dove, and lighting upon him:

AND LO a voice from heaven, saying, This is my beloved Son, in whom I am well pleased.

St Matthew
Chapter 4, verses 1-11

THEN WAS Jesus led up of the spirit into the wilderness to be
tempted of the devil.

AND WHEN he had fasted forty days and forty nights, he was
afterward an hungred.

AND WHEN the tempter came to him, he said, If thou be the Son
of God, command that these stones be made bread.

BUT HE answered and said . . . Man shall not live by bread alone,
but by every word that proceedeth out of the mouth of God.

THEN THE devil taketh him up into the holy city,
and setteth him on a pinnacle of the temple,

AND SAITH unto him, If thou be the Son of God, cast thyself
down: for it is written, He shall give his angels charge concerning thee . .

JESUS SAID unto him . . . Thou shalt not tempt the Lord thy God.

AGAIN, THE devil taketh him up into an exceeding high
mountain, and sheweth him all the kingdoms of the world,
and the glory of them;

AND SAITH unto him, All these things will I give thee, if thou
wilt fall down and worship me.

THEN SAITH Jesus unto him, Get thee hence, Satan: for it is
written, Thou shalt worship the Lord thy God, and him only
shalt thou serve.

THEN THE devil leaveth him, and, behold, angels came and
ministered unto him.

St Luke
Chapter 4, verses 16-21

AND HE came to Nazareth, where he had been brought up: and, as his custom was, he went into the synagogue on the sabbath day, and stood up for to read.

AND THERE was delivered unto him the book of the prophet Esaias. And when he opened the book, he found the place where it was written,

THE SPIRIT of the Lord is upon me, because he hath anointed me to preach the gospel to the poor; he hath sent me to heal the brokenhearted, to preach deliverance to the captives, and recovering of sight to the blind, to set at liberty them that are bruised,

TO PREACH the acceptable year of the Lord.

AND HE closed the book, and he gave it again to the minister, and sat down. And the eyes of all them that were in the synagogue were fastened on him.

AND HE began to say unto them, This day is this scripture fulfilled in your ears.

. . . they forsook all, and followed him
St Luke
Chapter 5, verses 1-11

AND IT came to pass, that, as the people pressed upon him to hear the word of God, he stood by the lake of Gennesaret,

AND SAW two ships standing by the lake: but the fishermen were gone out of them, and were washing their nets.

AND HE entered into one of the ships, which was Simon's, and prayed him that he would thrust out a little from the land. And he sat down, and taught the people out of the ship.

NOW WHEN he had left speaking, he said unto Simon, Launch out into the deep, and let down your nets for a draught.

AND SIMON answering said unto him, Master, we have toiled all the night, and have taken nothing: nevertheless at thy word I will let down the net.

AND WHEN they had this done, they inclosed a great multitude of fishes: and their net brake.

AND THEY beckoned unto their partners, which were in the other ship, that they should come and help them. And they came, and filled both the ships, so that they began to sink.

WHEN SIMON Peter saw it, he fell down at Jesus' knees, saying, Depart from me; for I am a sinful man, O Lord.

FOR HE was astonished, and all that were with him, at the draught of the fishes which they had taken:

AND SO was also James, and John, the sons of Zebedee, which were partners with Simon. And Jesus said unto Simon, Fear not; from henceforth thou shalt catch men.

AND WHEN they had brought their ships to land, they forsook all, and followed him.

St John

Chapter 2, verses 1-11

AND THE third day there was a marriage in Cana of Galilee; and the mother of Jesus was there:

AND BOTH Jesus was called, and his disciples, to the marriage.

AND WHEN they wanted wine, the mother of Jesus saith unto him, They have no wine.

JESUS SAITH unto her, Woman, what have I to do with thee? mine hour is not yet come.

HIS MOTHER saith unto the servants, Whatsoever he saith unto you, do it.

AND THERE were set there six waterpots of stone, after the manner of the purifying of the Jews, containing two or three firkins apiece.

JESUS SAITH unto them, Fill the waterpots with water. And they filled them up to the brim.

AND HE saith unto them, Draw out now, and bear unto the governor of the feast. And they bear it.

WHEN THE ruler of the feast had tasted the water that was made wine, and knew not whence it was: (but the servants which drew the water knew;) the governor of the feast called the bridegroom,

AND SAITH unto him, Every man at the beginning doth set forth good wine; and when men have well drunk, then that which is worse: but thou hast kept the good wine until now.

THIS BEGINNING of miracles did Jesus in Cana of Galilee, and manifested forth his glory; and his disciples believed on him.

St Mark

Chapter 1, verses 40-45

AND THERE came a leper to him, beseeching him, and kneeling down to him, and saying unto him, If thou wilt, thou canst make me clean.

AND JESUS, moved with compassion, put forth his hand, and touched him, and saith unto him, I will; be thou clean.

AND AS soon as he had spoken, immediately the leprosy departed from him, and he was cleansed.

AND HE straitly charged him, and forthwith sent him away;

AND SAITH unto him, See thou say nothing to any man: but go thy way, shew thyself to the priest, and offer for thy cleansing those things which Moses commanded, for a testimony unto them.

BUT HE went out, and began to publish it much, and to blaze abroad the matter, insomuch that Jesus could no more openly enter into the city, but was without in desert places: and they came to him from every quarter.

HEALTH AND HEALING

Health, cleanliness and hygiene were vitally important to the Jew of first-century Palestine. Cleanliness was considered a religious duty; man must respect his body as well as his soul for both were created in the divine likeness.

Cleanliness laws covered both the individual and the community. A man must take regular baths and always wash before eating; filthy and therefore disease-spreading housing was prohibited; the dietary laws were based on a desire to avoid food that was unclean. There is a rabbinic saying that 'three things do not enter the body, but it derives benefit therefrom: washing, anointing, and regular motions'. Moderation was advocated, and it was also said that 'In eight things excess is harmful and moderation beneficial: travel, sexual intercourse, wealth, work, wine sleep, hot water . . . and blood-letting.'

Yet despite these many steps taken to promote health, there was much disease in first-century Palestine. The New Testament mentions paralysis, epilepsy, blindness and eye disease (caused by the glaring sun and dust), deafness, fever (possibly forms of malaria and dysentery), and the dreaded leprosy. There are also many references to 'unclean spirits': like all ancient peoples, the Jews believed in evil spirits, who would possess a person and deprive him not only of his self control but also of his sense of right, thereby causing him to sin. Probably 'demonic possession' was really a type of mental illness, for example hysteria.

As health and cleanliness belonged to God's kingdom, so disease belonged to that of Satan. Illness was linked with evil, and often seen as the result of the sin of the sufferer or his parents. This was particularly so in the case of 'unclean' diseases such as leprosy which banned the sufferer from the community: even the Law could not help the leper.

If a person was ailing, it was therefore a religious duty to be restored to health. The physician was an important man in the community, though many were disliked as being too grasping or too lazy. Here are some typical remedies from the Talmud, using local herbs and food-stuffs: for fever, drink a jug of water, or eat meat cooked over glowing coals; for asthma, soak three wheat cakes in honey, and eat them in undiluted wine; for catarrh, drip milk over three cabbage stalks and stir it with marjoram; for a cataract, find a seven-coloured scorpion, grind it, and apply a certain amount of powder to the eye.

Many of these remedies have a strong element of the magical and superstitious, and in fact people often looked to the miraculous where ordinary medicine fell short. Acts of healing were performed by the rabbis, and wonder-workers abounded. Aside from the laying on of hands, many of the techniques were not very different from those used by physicians: for example the touching and manipulation of the affected organ, and the use of saliva or spittle. Exorcism of devils was also performed with a set form of incantation. Many places, such as the pool of Siloam in Jerusalem, were famed for their special curative powers.

In his own works of healing, Jesus uses techniques common to wonder-workers and physicians of his time. Yet contrary to common practice his miracles are not elaborate, and are often performed in private. He did not seek to draw attention to himself as a charismatic healer, but to God's saving and redemptive power that was being proclaimed through him to all creation. Victory over sickness was symbolic of a far wider victory over the forces of nature and of evil that was to inaugurate the Messianic age.

AND JESUS went about all Galilee, teaching in their synagogues, and preaching the gospel of the kingdom, and healing all manner of sickness and all manner of disease among the people.

AND HIS fame went throughout all Syria: and they brought unto him all sick people that were taken with divers diseases and torments, and those which were possessed with devils, and those which were lunatick, and those that had the palsy; and he healed them.

AND THERE followed him great multitudes of people from Galilee, and from Decapolis, and from Jerusalem, and from Judaea, and from beyond Jordan.

AND SEEING the multitudes, he went up into a mountain: and when he was set, his disciples came unto him:

AND HE opened his mouth, and taught them, saying,

BLESSED ARE the poor in spirit: for their's is the kingdom of heaven.

BLESSED ARE they that mourn: for they shall be comforted.

BLESSED ARE the meek: for they shall inherit the earth.

BLESSED ARE they which do hunger and thirst after righteousness: for they shall be filled.

BLESSED ARE the merciful: for they shall obtain mercy.

BLESSED ARE the pure in heart: for they shall see God.

BLESSED ARE the peacemakers: for they shall be called the children of God.

BLESSED ARE they which are persecuted for righteousness' sake: for their's is the kingdom of heaven.

BLESSED ARE ye, when men shall revile you, and persecute you, and shall say all manner of evil against you falsely, for my sake.

REJOICE, AND be exceeding glad: for great is your reward in heaven: for so persecuted they the prophets which were before you.

On marriage
St Matthew
Chapter 5, verses 27-28

YE HAVE heard that it was said by them of old time, Thou shalt not commit adultery:

BUT I say unto you, That whosoever looketh on a woman to lust after her hath committed adultery with her already in his heart.

On retribution
St Matthew
Chapter 5, verses 38-39

YE HAVE heard that it hath been said, An eye for an eye, and a tooth for a tooth:

BUT I say unto you, That ye resist not evil: but whosoever shall smite thee on thy right cheek, turn to him the other also.

On loving one's enemy
St Matthew
Chapter 5, verses 43-45

YE HAVE heard that it hath been said, Thou shalt love thy neighbour, and hate thine enemy.

BUT I say unto you, Love your enemies, bless them that curse you, do good to them that hate you, and pray for them which despitefully use you, and persecute you;

THAT YE may be the children of your Father which is in heaven: for he maketh his sun to rise on the evil and on the good, and sendeth rain on the just and on the unjust.

On his followers
St Matthew
Chapter 5, verses 14-16

YE ARE the light of the world. A city that is set on an hill cannot be hid.

NEITHER DO men light a candle, and put it under a bushel, but on a candlestick; and it giveth light unto all that are in the house.

LET YOUR light so shine before men, that they may see your good works, and glorify your Father which is in heaven.

On respect for the person
St Matthew
Chapter 5, verses 21-24

YE HAVE heard that it was said by them of old time, Thou shalt not kill; and whosoever shall kill shall be in danger of the judgment:

BUT I say unto you, That whosoever is angry with his brother without a cause shall be in danger of the judgment: and whosoever shall say to his brother, Raca, shall be in danger of the council: but whosoever shall say, Thou fool, shall be in danger of hell fire.

THEREFORE IF thou bring thy gift to the altar, and there rememberest that thy brother hath ought against thee;

LEAVE THERE thy gift before the altar, and go thy way; first be reconciled to thy brother, and then come and offer thy gift.

St Matthew

Chapter 6, verses 24-26

NO MAN can serve two masters: for either he will hate the one, and love the other; or else he will hold to the one, and despise the other. Ye cannot serve God and mammon.

THEREFORE I say unto you, Take no thought for your life, what ye shall eat, or what ye shall drink; not yet for your body, what ye shall put on. Is not the life more than meat, and the body than raiment?

BEHOLD THE fowls of the air: for they sew not, neither do they reap, nor gather into barns; yet your heavenly Father feedeth them. Are ye not much better than they?

On not passing judgment on others

St Luke

Chapter 6, verse 42

EITHER HOW canst thou say to thy brother, Brother, let me pull out the mote that is in thine eye, when thou thyself beholdst not the beam that is in thine own eye? Thou hypocrite, cast out first the beam out of thine own eye, and then shalt thou see clearly to pull out the mote that is in thy brother's eye.

On forgiveness

St Matthew

Chapter 18, verses 21-22

THEN CAME Peter to him, and said, Lord, how oft shall my brother sin against me, and I forgive him? till seven times?

JESUS SAITH unto him, I say not unto thee, Until seven times: but, Until seventy times seven.

On prayer

St Matthew

Chapter 6, verses 5-13

. . .WHEN THOU prayest, thou shalt not be as the hypocrites are: for they love to pray standing in the synogogues and in the corners of the streets, that they may be seen of men. Verily I say unto you, They have their reward.

BUT THOU, when thou prayest, enter into thy closet, and when thou hast shut thy door, pray to thy Father which is in secret; and thy Father which seeth in secret shall reward thee openly.

BUT WHEN ye pray, use not vain repetitions, as the heathens do: for they think that they shall be heard for their much speaking.

BE NOT ye therefore like unto them: for your Father knoweth what things ye have need of, before ye ask him.

AFTER THIS manner therefore pray ye: Our Father which art in heaven, Hallowed be thy name.

THY KINGDOM come. Thy will be done in earth, as it is in heaven.

GIVE US this day our daily bread.

AND LEAD us not into temptation, but deliver us from evil: For thine is the kingdom, and the power, and the glory, for ever. Amen.

On humility

St Luke

Chapter 14, verse 11

. . . WHOSOEVER EXALTETH himself shall be abased; and he that humbleth himself shall be exalted.

AND AGAIN he entered into Capernaum after some days; and it was noised that he was in the house.

AND STRAIGHTWAY many were gathered together, insomuch that there was no room to receive them, no, not so much as about the door: and he preached the word unto them.

AND THEY come unto him, bringing one sick of the palsy, which was borne of four.

AND WHEN they could not come nigh unto him for the press, they uncovered the roof where he was: and when they had broken it up, they let down the bed wherein the sick of the palsy lay.

WHEN JESUS saw their faith, he said unto the sick of the palsy, Son, thy sins be forgiven thee.

BUT THERE where certain of the scribes sitting there, and reasoning in their hearts,

WHY DOTH this man thus speak blasphemies? who can forgive sins but God only?

AND IMMEDIATELY when Jesus perceived in his spirit that they so reasoned within themselves, he said unto them, Why reason ye these thing in your hearts?

WHETHER IS it easier to say to the sick of the palsy, Thy sins be forgiven thee; or to say, Arise, and take up thy bed, and walk?

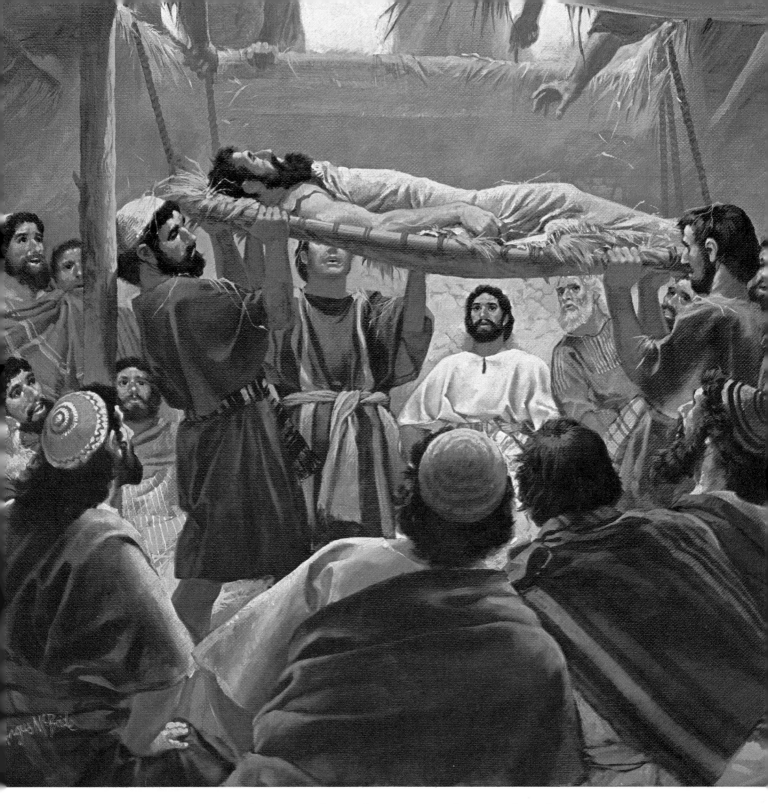

BUT THAT ye may know that the Son of man hath power on earth to forgive sins, (he saith to the sick of the palsy,)

I SAY unto thee, Arise, and take up thy bed, and go thy way into thine house.

AND IMMEDIATELY he arose, took up the bed, and went forth before them all; insomuch that they were all amazed, and glorified God, saying, We never saw it on this fashion.

St Luke

Chapter 5, verses 27-32

AND AFTER these things he went forth, and saw a publican, named Levi, sitting at the receipt of custom: and he said unto him, Follow me.

AND HE left all, rose up, and followed him.

AND LEVI made him a great feast in his own house: and there was a great company of publicans and of others that sat down with them.

BUT THEIR scribes and Pharisees murmured against his disciples, saying, Why do ye eat and drink with publicans and sinners?

AND JESUS answering said unto them, They that are whole need not a physician; but they that are sick.

I CAME NOT to call the righteous, but sinners to repentance.

THE SOCIAL OUTCASTS

Jesus turned in word and deed not to the socially respectable and orthodox, but to those set aside by the society of his time—the common people who 'heard him gladly'—and even to those on its very fringes: the tax-gatherers and sinners. Yet who were the people who came into this category?

The tax-gatherers were ordinary Jewish people who collaborated with the Romans by helping levy indirect taxes—and made a vast profit in the process. Seated by their custom-houses at such conspicuous places as entrances to towns, market places and cross-roads, they collected vast sums of money of which only a fixed amount had to be paid to the state. The rest went into their pockets. Needless to say, in a country where taxation was seen as one of the most vexing symbols of occupation, and where collaboration equalled apostasy, the tax-gatherer was an object of hatred.

It is possible that the term 'sinners' refers not only to those who had transgressed the moral law, such as the prostitutes, but also to the people who did not observe Mosaic Law—the *am-ha-aretz*. According to the Talmud, a man was *am-ha-aretz* if he did not 'eat his bread in a state of ritual cleanliness'. Initially designating the peasants who had settled in Israel while the Jews were in exile, and who were therefore regarded as usurpers, the term eventually came to be applied to all those, particularly workers and labourers, who had neither time nor inclination to study the Law, and who therefore neglected many of its numerous commands. In a religious and cultural environment which exhorted study as a means to holiness, they were regarded with suspicion and mistrust. The compassion of Jesus contrasts with the severity of the conventionally religious: he not only sought out and befriended the moral failures, he also ate with them—a most intimate gesture, and one which still implies peace and acceptance to all the peoples of the Middle East.

St Luke

Chapter 7, verses 36-50

AND ONE of the Pharisees desired him that he would eat with him. And he went into the Pharisee's house, and sat down to meat.

AND, BEHOLD, a woman in the city, which was a sinner, when she knew that Jesus sat at meat in the Pharisee's house, brought an alabaster box of ointment,

AND STOOD at his feet behind him weeping, and began to wash his feet with tears, and did wipe them with the hairs of her head, and kissed his feet, and anointed them with the ointment.

NOW WHEN the Pharisee which had bidden him saw it, he spake within himself, saying, This man, if he were a prophet, would have known who and what manner of woman this is that toucheth him: for she is a sinner.

AND JESUS answering said unto him, Simon, I have somewhat to say unto thee. And he saith, Master, say on.

THERE WAS a certain creditor which had two debtors: the one owed five hundred pence, and the other fifty.

AND WHEN they had nothing to pay, he frankly forgave them both. Tell me therefore, which of them will love him most?

SIMON ANSWERED and said, I suppose that he, to whom he forgave most. And he said unto him, Thou hast rightly judged.

AND HE turned to the woman, and said unto Simon, Seest thou this woman? I entered into thine house, thou gavest me no water for my feet: but she hath washed my feet with tears, and wiped them with the hairs of her head.

THOU GAVEST me no kiss: but this woman since the time I came in hath not ceased to kiss my feet.

MY HEAD with oil thou didst not anoint: but this woman hath anointed my feet with ointment.

WHEREFORE I say unto thee, Her sins, which are many, are forgiven; for she loved much: but to whom little is forgiven, the same loveth little.

AND HE said unto her, thy sins are forgiven.

AND THEY that sat at meat with him began to say within themselves, Who is this that forgiveth sins also?

AND HE said to the woman, Thy faith hath saved thee; go in peace.

The parable of the Prodigal Son
St Luke
Chapter 15, verses 11-24

AND HE said, A certain man had two sons:

AND THE younger of them said to his father, Father, give me the portion of goods that falleth to me. And he divided unto them his living.

AND NOT many days after the younger son gathered all together, and took his journey into a far country, and there wasted his substance with riotous living.

AND WHEN he had spent all, there arose a mighty famine in that land; and he began to be in want.

AND HE went and joined himself to a citizen of that country; and he sent him into his fields to feed swine.

AND HE would fain have filled his belly with the husks that the swine did eat: and no man gave unto him.

AND WHEN he came to himself, he said, How many hired servants of my father's have bread enough and to spare, and I perish with hunger!

I WILL arise and go to my father, and will say unto him, Father, I have sinned against heaven, and before thee,

AND AM no more worthy to be called thy son: make me as one of thy hired servants.

AND HE arose, and came to his father. But when he was yet a great way off, his father saw him, and had compassion, and ran, and fell on his neck, and kissed him.

AND THE son said unto him, Father, I have sinned against heaven, and in thy sight, and am no more worthy to be called thy son.

BUT THE father said to his servants, Bring forth the best robe, and put it on him; and put a ring on his hand, and shoes on his feet:

AND BRING hither the fatted calf, and kill it; and let us eat, and be merry:

FOR THIS my son was dead, and is alive again; he was lost, and is found. And they began to be merry.

St Mark

Chapter 4, verses 35-41

AND THE same day, when the even was come, he saith unto them, Let us pass over unto the other side.

AND WHEN they had sent away the multitude, they took him even as he was in the ship. And there were also with him other little ships.

AND THERE arose a great storm of wind, and the waves beat into the ship, so that it was now full.

AND HE was in the hinder part of the ship, asleep on a pillow: and they awake him, and say unto him, Master, carest thou not that we perish?

AND HE arose, and rebuked the wind, and said unto the sea, Peace, be still. And the wind ceased, and there was a great calm.

AND HE said unto them, Why are ye so fearful? how is it that ye have no faith?

AND THEY feared exceedingly, and said one to another, What manner of man is this, that even the wind and the sea obey him?

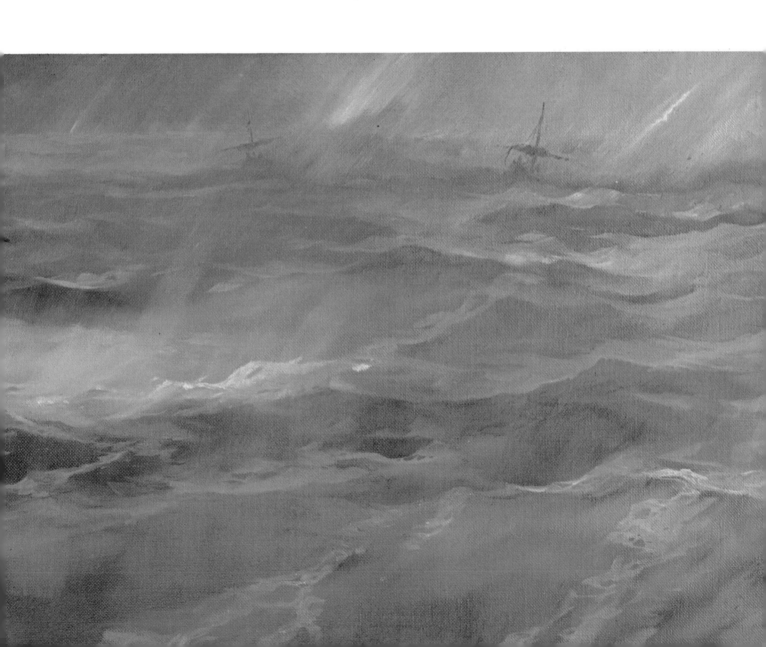

St Mark

Chapter 5, verses 1-13

AND THEY came over unto the other side of the sea, into the country of the Gadarenes.

AND WHEN he was come out of the ship, immediately there met him out of the tombs a man with an unclean spirit,

WHO HAD his dwelling among the tombs; and no man could bind him, no, not with chains:

BECAUSE THAT he had been often bound with fetters and chains, and the chains had been plucked asunder by him, and the fetters broken in pieces: neither could any man tame him.

AND ALWAYS, night and day, he was in the mountains, and in the tombs, crying, and cutting himself with stones.

BUT WHEN he saw Jesus afar off, he ran and worshipped him,

AND CRIED with a loud voice, and said, What have I to do with thee, Jesus, thou Son of the most high God? I adjure thee by God, that thou torment me not.

FOR HE said unto him, Come out of the man, thou unclean spirit.

AND HE asked him, What is thy name? And he answered, saying, My name is Legion: for we are many.

AND HE besought him much that he would not send them away out of the country.

NOW THERE was there nigh unto the mountains a great herd of swine feeding.

AND ALL the devils besought him, saying, Send us into the swine, that we may enter into them.

AND FORTHWITH Jesus gave them leave. And the unclean spirits went out, and entered into the swine: and the herd ran violently down a steep place into the sea, (they were about two thousand;) and were choked in the sea.

St Mark

Chapter 5, verses 22-34

AND, BEHOLD, there cometh one of the rulers of the synagogue, Jairus by name; and when he saw him, he fell at his feet,

AND BESOUGHT him greatly, saying, My little daughter lieth at the point of death: I pray thee, come and lay thy hands on her, that she may be healed; and she shall live.

AND JESUS went with him; and much people followed him, and thronged him.

AND A certain woman, which had an issue of blood twelve years,

AND HAD suffered many things of many physicians, and had spent all that she had, and was nothing bettered, but rather grew worse,

WHEN SHE had heard of Jesus, came in the press behind, and touched his garment.

FOR SHE said, If I may touch but his clothes, I shall be whole.

AND STRAIGHTWAY the fountain of her blood was dried up; and she felt in her body that she was healed of that plague.

AND JESUS, immediately knowing in himself that virtue had gone out of him, turned him about in the press, and said, Who touched my clothes?

AND HIS disciples said unto him, Thou seest the multitude thronging thee, and sayest thou, Who touched me?

AND HE looked round about to see her that had done this thing.

BUT THE woman fearing and trembling, knowing what was done in her, came and fell down before him, and told him all the truth.

AND HE said unto her, Daughter, thy faith hath made thee whole; go in peace, and be whole of thy plague.

Jesus raises Jairus' daughter
St Mark
Chapter 5, verses 35-43

WHILE HE yet spake, there came from the ruler of the synagogue's house certain which said, Thy daughter is dead: why troublest thou the Master any further?

AS SOON as Jesus heard the word that was spoken, he saith unto the ruler of the synagogue, Be not afraid, only believe.

AND HE suffered no man to follow him, save Peter, and James, and John the brother of James.

AND HE cometh to the house of the ruler of the synagogue, and seeth the tumult, and them that wept and wailed greatly.

AND WHEN he was come in, he saith unto them, Why make ye this ado, and weep? the damsel is not dead, but sleepeth.

AND THEY laughed him to scorn. But when he had put them all out, he taketh the father and the mother of the damsel, and them that were with him, and entereth in where the damsel was lying.

AND HE took the damsel by the hand, and said unto her, Talitha-cumi; which is, being interpreted, Damsel, I say unto thee, arise.

AND STRAIGHTWAY the damsel arose, and walked; for she was of the age of twelve years. And they were astonished with a great astonishment.

AND HE charged them straitly that no man should know it; and commanded that something should be given her to eat.

St Mark

Chapter 2, verses 23-28

AND IT came to pass, that he went
through the corn fields on the sabbath
day; and his disciples began, as they
went, to pluck the ears of corn.

AND THE Pharisees said unto him, Behold,
why do they on the sabbath day that
which is not lawful?

AND HE said unto them, Have ye never
read what David did, when he had need,
and was an hungred, he, and they that
were with him?

HOW HE went into the house of God in
the days of Abiathar the high priest, and
did eat the shewbread, which is not
lawful to eat but for the priests, and gave
also to them which were with him?

AND HE said unto them, The sabbath was
made for man, and not man for
the sabbath.

THEREFORE THE Son of man is Lord also
of the sabbath.

THE LAW

The giving of the Law to Moses on Mount Sinai marked the second stage in God's salvation of mankind through Israel. It solidified the covenant made with Abraham, created a sense of awe in the mind of the Jewish people, and was the first expression of ethical monotheism.

The Law consisted of the Ten Commandments, and an additional 613 precepts intended as a means and rule of worship and conduct. All these were written down in the first five books of the Bible (the Pentateuch) and were referred to as the Written Law or the Torah. 'Torah' means not only the Law but also the entire content of revelation as found in the Bible.

Although the Torah has many points of similarity with the Babylonian Code of Hammurabi, it possesses a unique place in the history of religion in that it is the first endeavour to link religion with morality, both personal and social. Idolatry is forbidden and monotheism promoted; righteousness and justice is upheld as the basis of all human conduct. Social as well as personal morality is covered: the rights of the labourer and of the slave are established; the non-Hebrew stranger is to be welcomed and treated as the equal of the Jew.

In the attempt to keep it relevant to people in changed economic, political and social circumstances, there grew up and oral commentary on the Written Law. Approximately 1000 years after the Sinai revelation, during the Babylonian exile, Jewish scribes set to work to try to make the Law more accessible to ordinary people. Gradually a set of rules, known as *hermeneutics*, was evolved, with the aid of which the Law could be examined and developed without violation of scriptural precepts. Later, after the destruction of the Jewish Temple in AD 70, the 'Oral Law' became written down in the Talmud, which itself became the vehicle for much discussion.

The Law was thus not something fixed for all time, but a living God-given tradition which must be constantly re-assessed to suit the demands of life. As time advanced, the scribes sought to bring more of life under its influence.

From its inception the Law had social implications; around the time of the Second Temple the entire Jewish nation was, within the confines of Caesar, governed by the precepts of the Law. For the average Jew, religion, in the form of the Law, permeated all areas of life. He must scrupulously observe the Sabbath and the Feasts, and pray at fixed times of the day wherever he might be; whom he could, and could not marry, was dictated by the Torah, as was his position in the family; he was forbidden to make his servant work for more than ten hours a day, and if he was himself a hired labourer his wages must be paid before sunset and his hours and conditions of work were laid down by the Law; if he had a problem with property, or wanted to sue for damages, it was to his rabbi that he turned for legal advice; cleanliness was rigorously exhorted, and to eat first without washing was regarded with great horror.

Thus was the Law meticulously extended to penetrate all aspects of everyday life.

Jesus himself was a devout Jew, worshipping in the Temple and observing Jewish feasts and customs. He acknowledged the God-given status of the Law. Yet he was profoundly aware that the Law might become legalism, and obedience to the letter rather than to the spirit, a devotion to externals rather than to essentials. If a man was ill on the Sabbath, should he not be cured even if it involved infringing Sabbath Law? Like the prophets before him, he reminded people that mercy, justice, love and humanity were more important than purity regulations.

The ideal of love of one's neighbour as the sum total of the Law was firmly rooted in Jewish ethical teaching. Jesus reinforced this teaching and, by forbidding retaliation and urging love of sinners—whom he constantly sought out in person—and even the enemy, he added to it and deepened it, bringing the Law to its fulfilment.

St Luke
Chapter 6, verses 6-12

AND IT came to pass also on another sabbath, that he entered into the synagogue and taught: and there was a man whose right hand was withered.

AND THE scribes and Pharisees watched him, whether he would heal on the sabbath day; that they might find an accusation against him.

BUT HE knew their thoughts, and said to the man which had the withered hand, Rise up, and stand forth in the midst. And he arose and stood forth.

THEN SAID Jesus unto them, I will ask you one thing; Is it lawful on the sabbath days to do good, or to do evil? to save life, or to destroy it?

AND LOOKING round about upon them all, he said unto the man, Stretch forth thy hand. And he did so: and his hand was restored whole as the other.

AND THEY were filled with madness; and communed one with another what they might do to Jesus.

AND IT came to pass in those days, that he went out into a mountain to pray, and continued all night in prayer to God.

AND, BEHOLD, a certain lawyer stood up, and tempted him, saying, Master, what shall I do to inherit eternal life?

HE SAID unto him, What is written in the law? how readest thou?

AND HE answering said, Thou shalt love the Lord thy God with all thy heart, and with all thy soul, and with all thy strength, and with all thy mind; and thy neighbour as thyself.

BUT HE, willing to justify himself, said unto Jesus, And who is my neighbour?

AND JESUS answering said, A certain man went down from Jerusalem to Jericho, and fell among thieves, which stripped him of his raiment, and wounded him, and departed, leaving him half dead.

AND BY chance there came down a certain priest that way: and when he saw him, he passed by on the other side.

AND LIKEWISE a Levite, when he was at the place, came and looked on him, and passed by on the other side.

BUT A certain Samaritan, as he journeyed, came where he was: and when he saw him, he had compassion on him,

AND WENT to him, and bound up his wounds, pouring in oil and wine, and set him on his own beast, and brought him to an inn, and took care of him.

AND ON the morrow when he departed, he took out two pence, and gave them to the host, and said unto him, Take care of him; and whatsoever thou spendest more, when I come again, I will repay thee.

WHICH NOW of these three, thinkest thou, was neighbour unto him that fell among the thieves?

AND HE said, He that shewed mercy on him. Then said Jesus unto him, Go, and do thou likewise.

St Matthew
Chapter 11, verses 2-6

NOW WHEN John had heard in the prison the
works of Christ, he sent two of his disciples,

AND SAID unto him, Art thou he that
should come, or do we look for another?

JESUS ANSWERED and said unto them, Go
and shew John again those things which
ye do hear and see:

THE BLIND receive their sight, and the lame
walk, the lepers are cleansed, and the deaf
hear, the dead are raised up, and the poor
have the gospel preached to them.

AND BLESSED is he, whosoever shall not be
offended in me.

THE DEAD SEA SCROLLS
AND THE ESSENES

Of the four main religious groups at the time of Jesus—the Pharisees, the Sadducees, the Zealots and the Essenes—comparatively little was known of the last group until one of the most remarkable archaeological discoveries of this century.

In 1947 an Arab shepherd stumbled across some jars containing scrolls wrapped in cloth and hidden in the recesses of the cliffs of the Dead Sea. When it was realized that these were likely to be Essene documents, a new interest in this group was aroused. Shortly afterwards, on the desolate, barren plateau of the Dead Sea, at a place named Khirbet Qumran, archaeological investigations were started to unearth the secrets of this mysterious group who had, with their precious library, fled to the caves almost twenty centuries ago. Excavations revealed not only more scrolls, but also a settlement consisting of large halls, a library, a refectory, a kitchen, a farm, large baths, and a council chamber: the settlement of the Qumran community, now almost universally believed to have consisted of Essenes.

The Essenes emerged after the Maccabaean revolt, when they refused either compromise with or armed revolt against the occupying powers: they fled from the world and went to live in an exclusive community based on the ideals of the common life, asceticism and obedience. They believed separation to be essential in order to be God's holy people, the true Israel. To this end they shunned not only the wicked and the heathen, but also other Jews who did not share their ideals; they lived in strict observance of the Law, carrying their interpretation of it to extremes (they refused for example to do *any* work on the Sabbath). Their leader was the Teacher of Righteousness, who was seen as a prophet with a divine mission to interpret the secrets of God's wisdom to his followers. Obtaining their salvation through the Law, the Essenes waited for the Messianic age when they, the sons of light, would help inaugurate the Kingdom of God by fighting against the wicked, the sons of darkness.

The practices of the Qumran community were based on the Essenes' belief that they were a priestly élite waiting for the Kingdom of God. They held regular assemblies for worship, which comprised study of the Bible and prayer. The Law was observed down to the smallest detail; all sinners were avoided. Asceticism was prized, as was chastity for the reason that a man could thereby avoid the contamination of intercourse. (Marriage was allowed but only for the purposes of procreation.) Ritual baths were regularly taken to ensure cleanliness and purity; a ritual meal based on the Passover feast was eaten in common as part of the liturgical worship. The community was characterized by its adherence to rigid rules: it had a strict hierarchy and a punctiliously observed liturgy.

There can be no doubt that some of the Essenes attained a high degree of holiness, nor that they were devoted to the essentials of Judaism. But they were totally divorced from the pressures and frustrations of life, and in their secluded monasteries they gave themselves up to strange visions—which the barren and lonely landscape must have fostered—in which they took part in a great cosmic drama fighting on the side of good against evil. Some of their beliefs and practices—and the sheer novelty of our knowledge of them—has led to many parallels being drawn between Essenism and Christianity, and even to the suggestion that Jesus may have been an Essene. Although there are many parallels, the differences are too many and too great to suppose any close connection. For example, Jesus' flexibility with regard to the Law contrasts strongly with Essenic rigidity; his constant and compassionate searching out of sinners with the segregation from the world and repudiation of the wicked of the desert sect. Jesus, who was accused of being a 'glutton and a winebibber' (Matt. 11.19)

was not an ascetic, nor did he advocate asceticism; he was moreover opposed to élitism and opened his message to all. For him, purity of heart counted more than ritual purity; far from renouncing the world, he constantly entered into conflict and communion with it.

The Essenes fought in the AD 66–70 war against the Romans alongside the Zealots. Seeing themselves as revolutionaries in the supernatural rather than the actual world order, they were instructed by a special 'war scroll' on the conduct of a holy war. When the Romans advanced towards the Qumran, they fled to the caves with their scrolls. Most of them perished, yet something of their spirit remained alive in Christian monasticism: devotion to a rule and renunciation of the world as a means of gaining holiness.

St Matthew

Chapter 10, verses 1-10

AND WHEN he had called unto him his twelve disciples, he gave them power against unclean spirits, to cast them out, and to heal all manner of sickness and all manner of disease.

NOW THE names of the twelve apostles are these; The first, Simon, who is called Peter, and Andrew his brother; James the son of Zebedee, and John his brother;

PHILIP, AND Bartholomew; Thomas, and Matthew the publican; James the son of Alphaeus, and Lebbaeus, whose surname was Thaddaeus;

SIMON THE Canaanite, and Judas Iscariot, who also betrayed him.

THESE TWELVE Jesus sent forth, and commanded them, saying, Go not into the way of the Gentiles, and into any city of the Samaritans enter ye not:

BUT GO rather to the lost sheep of the house of Israel.

AND AS ye go, preach, saying, The kingdom of heaven is at hand.

HEAL THE sick, cleanse the lepers, raise the dead, cast out devils: freely ye have received, freely give.

PROVIDE NEITHER gold, nor silver, nor brass in your purses,

NOR SCRIP for your journey, neither two coats, neither shoes, nor yet staves: for the workman is worthy of his meat.

The sayings of Jesus as reported by Matthew, Mark and Luke reveal a man with a powerful poetic imagination, and an awareness of the beauties of nature and its harmony with man.

St Matthew

Chapter 6, verses 26, 28

BEHOLD THE fowls of the air: for they sow not, neither do they reap, nor gather into barns; yet your heavenly Father feedeth them. Are ye not much better than they?

AND WHY take ye thought for raiment? Consider the lilies of the field, how they grow; they toil not, neither do they spin.

St Luke

Chapter 8, verses 5-8

A SOWER went out to sow his seed: and as he sowed, some fell by the way side; and it was trodden down, and the fowls of the air devoured it.

AND SOME fell upon a rock; and as soon as it was sprung up, it withered away, because it lacked moisture.

AND SOME fell among thorns; and the thorns sprang up with it, and choked it.

AND OTHER fell on good ground, and sprang up, and bare fruit an hundredfold.

St Matthew

Chapter 10, verse 29

ARE NOT two sparrows sold for a farthing? and one of them shall not fall on the ground without your Father.

He prefers the image to the abstract saying.

St Luke

Chapter 6, verse 38

GIVE, AND it shall be given unto you; good measure, pressed down, and shaken together, and running over, shall men give into your bosom. For with the same measure that ye mete withal it shall be measured to you again.

St Mark

Chapter 4, verses 26-32

AND HE said, So is the kingdom of God, as if a man should cast seed into the ground;

AND SHOULD sleep, and rise night and day, and the seed should spring and grow up, he knoweth not how.

FOR THE earth bringeth forth fruit of herself; first the blade, then the ear, after that the full corn in the ear.

BUT WHEN the fruit is brought forth, immediately he putteth in the sickle, because the harvest is come.

AND HE said, Whereunto shall we liken the kingdom of God? or with what comparison shall we compare it?

IT IS like a grain of mustard seed, which, when it is sown in the earth, is less than all the seeds that be in the earth:

BUT WHEN it is sown, it groweth up, and becometh greater than all herbs, and shooteth out great branches; so that the fowls of the air may lodge under the shadow of it.

St Luke
Chapter 13, verses 18-19

THEN SAID he, Unto what is the kingdom of God like? and whereunto shall I resemble it?

IT IS like a grain of mustard seed, which a man took, and cast into his garden; and it grew, and waxed a great tree; and the fowls of the air lodged in the branches of it.

St Luke
Chapter 11, verses 33-34

NO MAN, when he hath lighted a candle, putteth it in a secret place, neither under a bushel, but on a candlestick, that they which come in may see the light.

THE LIGHT of the body is the eye: therefore when thine eye is single, thy whole body also is full of light; but when thine eye is evil, thy body also is full of darkness.

The imagery that John ascribes to Jesus is more direct: a few standard themes, such as bread, light, water, serve as leitmotifs throughout the gospel and are used to illustrate Jesus' relationship with God and man.

St John
Chapter 15, verses 1-5

I AM the true vine, and my Father is the husbandman.

EVERY BRANCH in me that beareth not fruit he taketh away: and every branch that beareth fruit, he purgeth it, that it may bring forth more fruit.

NOW YE are clean through the word which I have spoken unto you.

ABIDE IN me, and I in you. As the branch cannot bear fruit of itself, except it abide in the vine; no more can ye, except ye abide in me.

I AM the vine, ye are the branches: He that abideth in me, and I in him, the same bringeth forth much fruit: for without me ye can do nothing.

St John
Chapter 8, verse 12

THEN SPAKE Jesus again unto them, saying, I am the light of the world: he that followeth me shall not walk in darkness, but shall have the light of life.

St John
Chapter 6, verses 35-51

AND JESUS said unto them, I am the bread of life: he that cometh to me shall never hunger; and he that believeth in me shall never thirst.

I AM the living bread which came down from heaven: if any man eat of this bread, he shall live for ever: and the bread that I will give is my flesh, which I will give for the life of the world.

St John
Chapter 10, verse 11

I AM the good shepherd: the good shepherd giveth his life for the sheep.

St Luke
Chapter 10, verses 38-42

NOW IT came to pass, as they went, that he entered into a certain village: and a certain woman named Martha received him into her house.

AND SHE had a sister called Mary, which also sat at Jesus' feet, and heard his word.

BUT MARTHA was cumbered about much serving, and came to him, and said, Lord, dost thou not care that my sister hath left me to serve alone? bid her therefore that she help me.

AND JESUS answered and said unto her, Martha, Martha, thou art careful and troubled about many things:

BUT ONE thing is needful: and Mary hath chosen that good part, which shall not be taken away from her.

WOMEN IN ISRAEL

The status of Jewish women was relatively high, compared with that among other people of the ancient world. The family was held sacred due to the importance of maintaining the dynasty; it was also the basic unit on which society depended. The married woman was deemed mistress of her household, as her husband was its lord: her duties were to provide food and clothing for her family, as well as to grind flour, bake, launder, cook, nurse her children, make the beds, and spin well; she might sometimes help her husband in the fields, and even earn a small living through the practice of crafts and horticulture. In addition, she was responsible for hospitality to the traveller (vital in the absence of inns) and gave alms to the poor. A beautiful description of the ideal wife is given in Proverbs 31: 10–31.

Yet despite their great responsibilities, women were in some ways restricted. Although they were allowed out of their homes, they were required always to behave modestly and men were forbidden to speak with them. A man could divorce his wife simply by giving her a note of dismissal for such reasons as childlessness, adultery (for which she could be stoned to death), or even, according to some, bad housekeeping. For the woman, divorce was virtually impossible. Women were not allowed beyond a certain court in the Temple, nor were they required to study the Torah.

Women were among the closest friends and companions of Jesus. He approached them without reserve, was at ease in their company, even discussing theology with them. By prohibiting divorce for *both* sexes, he in fact enhanced their status, making them the definitive equals of men.

Jesus with women: the meeting
with the Samaritan woman at the well

St John

Chapter 4, verses 5-26

THEN COMETH he to a city of Samaria, which is called Sychar, near to the parcel of ground that Jacob gave to his son Joseph.

NOW JACOB'S well was there. Jesus therefore, being wearied with his journey, sat thus on the well: and it was about the sixth hour.

THERE COMETH a woman of Samaria to draw water: Jesus saith unto her, Give me to drink.

(FOR HIS disciples were gone away unto the city to buy meat.)

THEN SAITH the woman of Samaria unto him, How is it that thou, being a Jew, askest drink of me, which am a woman of Samaria? for the Jews have no dealings with the Samaritans.

JESUS ANSWERED and said unto her, If thou knewest the gift of God, and who it is that saith to thee, Give me to drink; thou wouldest have asked of him, and he would have given thee living water.

THE WOMAN saith unto him, Sir, thou hast nothing to draw with, and the well is deep: from whence then hast thou that living water?

ART THOU greater than our father Jacob, which gave us the well, and drank thereof himself, and his children, and his cattle?

JESUS ANSWERED and said unto her, Whosoever drinketh of this water shall thirst again:

BUT WHOSOEVER drinketh of the water that I shall give him shall never thirst; but the water that I shall give him shall be in him a well of water springing up into everlasting life.

THE WOMAN saith unto him, Sir give me this water, that I thirst not, neither come hither to draw.

JESUS SAITH unto her, Go, call thy husband, and come hither.

THE WOMAN answered and said, I have no husband. Jesus said unto her, Thou hast well said, I have no husband:

FOR THOU hast had five husbands; and he whom thou now hast is not thy husband: in that saidst thou truly.

THE WOMAN saith unto him, Sir, I perceive that thou art a prophet.

OUR FATHERS worshipped in this mountain; and ye say, that in Jerusalem is the place where men ought to worship.

JESUS SAITH unto her, Woman, believe me, the hour cometh, when ye shall neither in this mountain, nor yet at Jerusalem, worship the Father.

YE WORSHIP ye know not what: we know what we worship: for salvation is of the Jews.

BUT THE hour cometh, and now is, when the true worshippers shall worship the Father in spirit and in truth: for the Father seeketh such to worship him.

GOD IS a Spirit: and they that worship him must worship him in spirit and in truth.

THE WOMAN saith unto him, I know that Messias cometh, which is called Christ: when he is come, he will tell us all things.

JESUS SAITH unto her, I that speak unto thee am he.

A Roman centurion asks that his servant may be healed

St Matthew
Chapter 8, verses 5-10; 13

AND WHEN Jesus was entered into Capernaum, there came unto him a centurion, beseeching him,

AND SAYING, Lord, my servant lieth at home sick of the palsy, grievously tormented.

AND JESUS saith unto him, I will come and heal him.

THE CENTURION answered and said, Lord, I am not worthy that thou shouldest come under my roof: but speak the word only, and my servant shall be healed.

FOR I am a man under authority, having soldiers under me: and I say to this man, Go, and he goeth; and to another, Come, and he cometh; and to my servant, Do this, and he doeth it.

WHEN JESUS heard it, he marvelled, and said to them that followed, Verily I say unto you, I have not found so great faith, no, not in Israel.

AND JESUS said unto the centurion, Go thy way; and as thou hast believed, so be it done unto thee. And his servant was healed in the selfsame hour.

St Matthew

Chapter 14, verses 3-12

FOR HEROD had laid hold on John, and bound him, and put him in prison for Herodias' sake, his brother Philip's wife.

FOR JOHN said unto him, It is not lawful for thee to have her.

AND WHEN he would have put him to death, he feared the multitude, because they counted him as a prophet.

BUT WHEN Herod's birthday was kept, the daughter of Herodias danced before them, and pleased Herod.

WHEREUPON HE promised with an oath to give her whatsoever she would ask.

AND SHE, being before instructed of her mother, said, Give me here John Baptist's head in a charger.

AND THE king was sorry: nevertheless for the oath's sake, and them which sat with him at meat, he commanded it to be given her.

AND HE sent, and beheaded John in the prison.

AND HIS head was brought in a charger, and given to the damsel: and she brought it to her mother.

AND HIS disciples came, and took up the body, and buried it, and went and told Jesus.

St John
Chapter 6, verses 1-15

AFTER THESE things Jesus went over the sea of Galilee, which is the sea of Tiberias.

AND A great multitude followed him, because they saw his miracles which he did on them that were diseased.

AND JESUS went up into a mountain, and there he sat with his disciples.

AND THE passover, a feast of the Jews, was nigh.

WHEN JESUS then lifted up his eyes, and saw a great company come unto him, he saith unto Philip, Whence shall we buy bread, that these may eat?

AND THIS he said to prove him: for he himself knew what he would do.

PHILIP ANSWERED him, Two hundred pennyworth of bread is not sufficient for them, that every one of them may take a little.

ONE OF his disciples, Andrew, Simon Peter's brother, saith unto him,

THERE IS a lad here, which hath five barley loaves, and two small fishes: but what are they among so many?

AND JESUS said, Make the men sit down. Now there was much grass in the place. So the men sat down, in number about five thousand.

AND JESUS took the loaves; and when he had given thanks, he distributed to the disciples, and the disciples to them that were set down; and likewise of the fishes as much as they would.

WHEN THEY were filled, he said unto his disciples, Gather up the fragments that remain, that nothing be lost.

THEREFORE THEY gathered them together, and filled twelve baskets with the fragments of the five barley loaves, which remained over and above unto them that had eaten.

THEN THOSE men, when they had seen the miracle that Jesus did, said, This is of a truth that prophet that should come into the world.

WHEN JESUS therefore perceived that they would come and take him by force, to make him a king, he departed again into a mountain himself alone.

LIFE OF CHRIST

. . . The saddest country in the world is perhaps the region round about Jerusalem. Galilee, on the contrary, was a very green, shady, smiling district, the true home of the Song of Songs, and the songs of the well-beloved. During the two months of March and April the country forms a carpet of flowers of an incomparable variety of colours. The animals are small and extremely gentle—delicate and lively turtle-doves, blue-birds so light that they rest on a blade of grass without bending it, crested larks which venture almost under the feet of the traveller, little river tortoises with mild and lively eyes, storks with grave and modest mien, which, laying aside all timidity, allow man to come quite near them, and seem almost to invite his approach. In no country in the world do the mountains spread themselves out with more harmony or inspire higher thoughts. Jesus seems to have had a peculiar love for them. The most important acts of his divine career took place upon the mountains. It was there that he was the most inspired; it was there that he held secret communion with the ancient prophets; and it was there that his disciples witnessed his transfiguration.

RENAN, *Life of Jesus*

ᎫESUS WENT unto the mount of Olives.

AND EARLY in the morning he came again into the temple, and all the people came unto him; and he sat down, and taught them.

AND THE scribes and Pharisees brought unto him a woman taken in adultery; and when they had set her in the midst,

THEY SAY unto him, Master, this woman was taken in adultery, in the very act.

NOW MOSES in the law commanded us, that such should be stoned: but what sayest thou?

THIS THEY said, tempting him, that they might have to accuse him. But Jesus stooped down, and with his finger wrote on the ground, as though he heard them not.

SO WHEN they continued asking him, he lifted up himself, and said unto them, He that is without sin among you, let him first cast a stone at her.

AND AGAIN he stooped down, and wrote on the ground.

AND THEY which heard it, being convicted by their own conscience, went out one by one, beginning at the eldest, even unto the last: and Jesus was left alone, and the woman standing in the midst.

WHEN JESUS had lifted up himself, and saw none but the woman, he said unto her, Woman, where are those thine accusers? hath no man condemned thee?

SHE SAID, No man, Lord. And Jesus said unto her, Neither do I condemn thee: go, and sin no more.

St John
Chapter 9, verses 1-7

AND AS Jesus passed by, he saw a man which was blind from his birth.

AND HIS disciples asked him, saying, Master, who did sin, this man, or his parents, that he was born blind?

JESUS ANSWERED, Neither hath this man sinned, nor his parents: but that the works of God should be made manifest in him.

I MUST work the works of him that sent me, while it is day: the night cometh, when no man can work.

AS LONG as I am in the world, I am the light of the world.

WHEN HE had thus spoken, he spat on the ground, and made clay of the spittle, and he anointed the eyes of the blind man with the clay,

AND SAID unto him, Go, wash in the pool of Siloam, (which is by interpretation, Sent.) He went his way therefore, and washed, and came seeing.

AND JESUS went out, and his disciples, into the towns of Caesarea Philippi: and by the way he asked his disciples, saying unto them, Whom do men say that I am?

AND THEY answered, John the Baptist: but some say, Elias, and others, One of the prophets.

AND HE saith unto them, But whom say ye that I am? And Peter answereth and saith unto him, Thou art the Christ.

AND HE charged them that they should tell no man of him.

THE MESSIAH

The word 'messiah' comes from the Hebrew *mash'iah*, meaning anointed. It originally denoted the special relationship between the king of the House of David and God: at his enthronement, the king became the divine representative, the intermediary between God and the community. When Israel was overwhelmingly defeated and her autonomy taken from her, her people looked towards one from the House of David who would restore her political power, and accomplish a supernatural victory of the forces of order against those of chaos.

After the disintegration of the kingdom in 586 BC, the spiritual leaders of Israel thus comforted their people with the Messianic hope. This hope was sometimes conceptualized as a kingly figure, the anointed one of Yahweh who would bring salvation. The Jewish people looked forward to a Golden Age when Israel's power would be restored and she would know peace, justice and abundance. Yet whether inaugurated by an individual or whether generalized as an era, the Messianic hope always contains the ideals of God's triumph over evil, the restoration of a just world order, and, above all, universality. The covenant made with Abraham will be brought to fruition, and salvation extended to all nations.

Yet there is sometimes another element in the depiction of the Messiah: that of suffering. This aspect is movingly portrayed by the prophet Isaiah in the figure of the Suffering Servant. Written at a time when the Jews were under captivity, the songs of the Servant give the assurance that Yahweh has not deserted his people, and that through him God will raise up Israel and extend his salvation to the Gentiles. The Servant's ministry has, despite his unique relationship with God, brought him in some unknown way into great suffering. Yet it is this suffering which has enabled him to serve: his life has become a vicarious offering for all mankind, he a 'man for others'. Many see this mysterious figure as an allegory for Israel; others as a prophet greater even than Moses who will universalize God's message and extend the covenant with Abraham to the Jews.

Several centuries later, around the time of the Maccabaean revolt, there emerged another concept of the Messiah, which first appears in the Book of Daniel. This figure is also God's anointed one who will bring about his kingdom: the difference however is that he will do this not in the context of history but at the end of time through supernatural intervention. Daniel describes him in highly symbolic terms as a redeemer figure of great might and power, to whom all worldly empires will pay homage. The Son of Man, as he is designated, also appears in the Apocrypha, where ideas of a political Messiah, intensified through many centuries of oppression, are focussed on this supernatural figure.

When the Romans succeeded the Seleucids as overlords of Israel, Jewish discontent reached fever pitch. Ideas on the Messiah, and expectations of his coming, proliferated as never before. In contemporary literature he is seen in different ways: as the traditional Son of David who will purge Israel of the heathen and of the sinner; as a superhuman being whose power is attested by the wonders he performs; and even as a more savage warlike figure who will introduce the Messianic kingdom by force, leaving a land strewn with the corpses of his enemies.

The Pharisees and the Sadducees showed little interest in the advent of the Messiah, the former working to bring about God's kingdom through prayer and observance of the Law. The Zealots looked for a national leader; the Essenes believed in the coming of two Messiahs, a priestly one and one of Davidic descent. Yet Messianic longings were probably strongest among the ordinary people—the poor, the underprivileged, the social rejects, the sick in body and mind—who longed for a liberator to release them from their hopeless condition.

Jesus' reluctance to declare himself openly as Messiah is understandable in the light of the unstable political circumstances of his time. To liberate his people in a direct sense would have nullified his message for subsequent generations, and linked it with a particular time, and regime, only. Yet both suffering and exaltation are inherent in Jesus' understanding of himself: he is both a 'man for others' and also the exalted Son of Man. When others came to understand the implications of this paradox, Jesus was seen more and more as Messiah not in one sense, but in many: as God's exalted Son, manifesting divine power, as the culmination of Old Testament hopes, as saviour of the poor and the oppressed, and above all, as God's ultimate revelation of himself.

AND HE began to teach them, that the Son of man must suffer many things, and be rejected of the elders, and of the chief priests, and scribes, and be killed, and after three days rise again.

AND HE spake that saying openly. And Peter took him, and began to rebuke him.

BUT WHEN he had turned about and looked on his disciples, he rebuked Peter, saying, Get thee behind me, Satan: for thou savourest not the things that be of God, but the things that be of men.

AND WHEN he had called the people unto him with his disciples also, he said unto them, Whosoever will come after me, let him deny himself, and take up his cross, and follow me.

FOR WHOSOEVER will save his life shall lose it; but whosoever shall lose his life for my sake and the gospel's, the same shall save it.

FOR WHAT shall it profit a man, if he shall gain the whole world, and lose his own soul?

OR WHAT shall a man give in exchange for his soul?

WHOSOEVER THEREFORE shall be ashamed of me and of my words in this adulterous and sinful generation; of him also shall the Son of man be ashamed, when he cometh in the glory of his Father with the holy angels.

AND IT came to pass about an eight days after these sayings, he took Peter and John and James, and went up into a mountain to pray.

AND AS he prayed, the fashion of his countenance was altered, and his raiment was white and glistering.

AND, BEHOLD, there talked with him two men, which were Moses and Elias:

WHO APPEARED in glory, and spake of his decease which he should accomplish at Jerusalem.

BUT PETER and they that were with him were heavy with sleep: and when they were awake, they saw his glory, and the two men that stood with him.

AND IT came to pass, as they departed from him, Peter said unto Jesus, Master, it is good for us to be here: and let us make three tabernacles; one for thee, and one for Moses, and one for Elias: not knowing what he said.

WHILE HE thus spake, there came a cloud, and overshadowed them: and he feared as they entered into the cloud.

AND THERE came a voice out of the cloud, saying, This is my beloved Son: hear him.

AND WHEN the voice was past, Jesus was found alone. And they kept it close, and told no man in those days any of those things which they had seen.

St Matthew
Chapter 18, verses 1-6

AT THE same time came the disciples unto Jesus, saying, Who is the greatest in the kingdom of heaven?

AND JESUS called a little child unto him, and set him in the midst of them,

AND SAID, Verily I say unto you, Except ye be converted, and become as little children, ye shall not enter into the kingdom of heaven.

WHOSOEVER THEREFORE shall humble himself as this little child, the same is greatest in the kingdom of heaven.

AND WHOSO shall receive one such little child in my name receiveth me.

BUT WHOSO shall offend one of these little ones which believe in me, it were better for him that a millstone were hanged about his neck, and that he were drowned in the depth of the sea.

AND WHEN he was gone forth into the way, there came one running, and kneeled to him, and asked him, Good Master, what shall I do that I may inherit eternal life?

AND JESUS said unto him, Why callest thou me good? there is none good but one, that is God.

THOU KNOWEST the commandments, Do not commit adultery, Do not kill, Do not steal, Do not bear false witness, Defraud not, Honour thy father and mother.

AND HE answered and said unto him, Master, all these have I observed from my youth.

THEN JESUS beholding him loved him, and said unto him, One thing thou lackest: go thy way, sell whatsoever thou hast, and give to the poor, and thou shalt have treasure in heaven: and come, take up the cross, and follow me.

AND HE was sad at that saying, and went away grieved: for he had great possessions.

AND JESUS looked round about, and saith unto his disciples, How hardly shall they that have riches enter into the kingdom of God!

AND THE disciples were astonished at his words. But Jesus answereth again, and saith unto them, Children, how hard is it for them that trust in riches to enter into the kingdom of God!

St Matthew
Chapter 11, verses 28-30

COME UNTO me, all ye that labour and are heavy laden, and I will give you rest.

TAKE MY yoke upon you, and learn of me; for I am meek and lowly in heart: and ye shall find rest unto your souls.

FOR MY yoke is easy, and my burden is light.

St Luke
Chapter 9, verses 57-62

AND IT came to pass, that, as they went in the way, a certain man said unto him, Lord, I will follow thee whithersoever thou goest.

AND JESUS said unto him, Foxes have holes, and birds of the air have nests; but the Son of man hath not where to lay his head.

AND HE said unto another, Follow me. But he said, Lord, suffer me first to go and bury my father.

JESUS SAID unto him, let the dead bury their dead: but go thou and preach the kingdom of God.

AND ANOTHER also said, Lord, I will follow thee; but let me first go bid them farewell, which are at home at my house.

AND JESUS said unto him, No man, having put his hand to the plough, and looking back, is fit for the Kingdom of God.

The raising of Lazarus

St John

Chapter 11, verses 1, 20-28, 32-45

NOW A certain man was sick, named Lazarus, of Bethany, the town of Mary and her sister Martha . . .

. . . THEN MARTHA, as soon as she heard that Jesus was coming, went and met him: but Mary sat still in the house.

THEN SAID Martha unto Jesus, Lord, if thou hadst been here, my brother had not died.

BUT I know, that even now, whatsoever thou wilt ask of God, God will give it thee.

JESUS SAITH unto her, Thy brother shall rise again.

MARTHA SAITH unto him, I know that he shall rise again in the resurrection at the last day.

JESUS SAID unto her, I am the resurrection, and the life: he that believeth in me, though he were dead, yet shall he live:

AND WHOSOEVER liveth and believeth in me shall never die. Believest thou this?

SHE SAITH unto him, Yea, Lord: I believe that thou are the Christ, the Son of God, which should come into the world.

AND WHEN she had so said, she went her way, and called Mary her sister secretly, saying, The Master is come, and calleth for thee . . .

. . . THEN WHEN Mary was come where Jesus was, and saw him, she fell down at his feet, saying unto him, Lord, if thou hadst been here, my brother had not died.

102

WHEN JESUS therefore saw her weeping, and the Jews also weeping which came with her, he groaned in the spirit, and was troubled.

AND SAID, Where have ye laid him? They said unto him, Lord, come and see.

JESUS WEPT.

THEN SAID the Jews, Behold how he loved him!

AND SOME of them said, Could not this man, which opened the eyes of the blind, have caused that even this man should not have died?

JESUS THEREFORE again groaning in himself cometh to the grave. It was a cave, and a stone lay upon it.

JESUS SAID, Take ye away the stone. Martha, the sister of him that was dead, saith unto him, Lord, by this time he stinketh: for he hath been dead four days.

JESUS SAITH unto her, Said I not unto thee, that, if thou wouldest believe, thou shouldest see the glory of God?

THEN THEY took away the stone from the place where the dead was laid. And Jesus lifted up his eyes, and said, Father, I thank thee that thou hast heard me.

AND I knew that thou hearest me always: but because of the people which stand by I said it, that they may believe that thou hast sent me.

AND WHEN he thus had spoken, he cried with a loud voice, Lazarus, come forth.

AND HE that was dead came forth, bound hand and foot with graveclothes: and his face was bound about with a napkin. Jesus saith unto them, Loose him, and let him go.

THEN MANY of the Jews which came to Mary, and had seen the things which Jesus did, believed on him.

St Luke
Chapter 19, verses 1-9

AND JESUS entered and passed through Jericho.

AND, BEHOLD, there was a man named Zacchaeus, which was the chief among the publicans, and he was rich.

AND HE sought to see Jesus who he was; and could not for the press, because he was little of stature.

AND HE ran before, and climbed up into a sycomore tree to see him: for he was to pass that way.

AND WHEN Jesus came to the place, he looked up, and saw him, and said unto him, Zacchaeus, make haste, and come down; for to day I must abide at thy house.

AND HE made haste, and came down, and received him joyfully.

AND WHEN they saw it, they all murmured, saying, That he was gone to be guest with a man that is a sinner.

AND ZACCHAEUS stood and said unto the Lord; Behold, Lord, the half of my goods I give to the poor; and if I have taken any thing from any man by false accusation, I restore him fourfold.

AND JESUS said unto him, This day is salvation come to this house, forsomuch as he also is a son of Abraham.

AND WHEN they came nigh to Jerusalem, unto Bethphage and Bethany, at the mount of Olives, he sendeth forth two of his disciples,

AND SAITH unto them, Go your way into the village over against you: and as soon as ye be entered into it, ye shall find a colt tied, whereon never man sat; loose him, and bring him.

AND IF any man say unto you, Why do ye this? say ye that the Lord hath need of him; and straightway he will send him hither.

AND THEY went their way, and found the colt tied by the door without in a place where two ways met; and they loose him . . .

... AND THEY brought the colt to Jesus, and cast their garments on him; and he sat upon him.

AND MANY spread their garments in the way: and others cut down branches off the trees, and strawed them in the way.

AND THEY that went before, and they that followed, cried, saying, Hosanna; Blessed is he that cometh in the name of the Lord:

BLESSED BE the kingdom of our father David, that cometh in the name of the Lord: Hosanna in the highest.

AND JESUS entered into Jerusalem, and into the temple: and when he had looked round about upon all things, and now the eventide was come, he went out unto Bethany with the twelve.

AND THEY come to Jerusalem: and Jesus went into the temple, and began to cast out them that sold and bought in the temple, and overthrew the tables of the moneychangers, and the seats of them that sold doves;

AND WOULD not suffer that any man should carry any vessel through the temple.

AND HE taught, saying unto them, Is it not written, My house shall be called of all nations the house of prayer? but ye have made it a den of thieves.

AND THE scribes and chief priests heard it, and sought how they might destroy him: for they feared him, because all the people was astonished at his doctrine.

THE TEMPLE

First built during the reign of Solomon, the Temple at Jerusalem represented the same spiritual haven that Mecca does for today's Muslim. Its inner sanctuary contained the Ark of the Covenant, and it provided a centre for prayer and sacrifice for as long as Israel remained independent.

The Temple was destroyed when the Jews were taken into captivity (586 BC), and rebuilt on their return (515 BC). During the Greek and Roman occupations it was subjected to a series of outrages: it was used as a sanctuary for Zeus, and was stormed by Pompey when he captured Jerusalem.

Herod the Great rebuilt the Temple in 20 BC in the Graeco-Roman style, making it one of the wonders of the ancient world. It was constructed on the principle of a progression to greater holiness, with a series of steps marking each stage in the ascent to the One God of Israel.

The first court was the court of the Gentiles, which served not only the foreigner but also all those who were for some reason unclean, who had offended against the Law. It was surrounded by graceful colonnades and overlooked the Mount of Olives and the Kidron Valley; and it was primarily a place for social gathering. Here also the money-changers, who changed foreign coins for ritually clean ones, and the sellers of animals for sacrifice, traded their wares amidst a great deal of noise which so insensed Jesus that he drove them out. From this court fifteen steps led up to the sanctuary, where only the Jews were allowed. The first court within this area was the court of women. Fifteen more steps lead up to the court of Israelites, the men's court. Another three gave on to the truly sacred area, where the High Priest blessed the people from the priests' court, and where sacrificial worship took place.

Another twelve steps led to the Sanctuary, the Holy of Holies, which was fifty feet up from the court of the Gentiles and 200 from the Kidron Valley. It was entered by a door of cedar covered in gold and hidden by a curtain. Inside was a long gallery panelled with cedar and cypress-wood and divided into two sections by another curtain. The first contained the shew-bread and other religious objects; the second was dark and bare, and it was here that the High Priest encountered God in the Holy of Holies.

The Temple was thus a supreme monument constructed by the Jews where they could gather for prayer and sacrificial worship based on penitence and thanksgiving. It was also the seat of the Sanhedrin, the supreme Jewish assembly, part lay, part priestly, who administered the law according to the precepts of the Torah. In many ways, the Temple was the epitome of the aspirations of Israel and the symbol of its national hopes. When it fell with the rest of Jerusalem in AD 70, it was the ending of an era in the history of Judaism as much as the demise of a nation.

St Matthew
Chapter 22, verses 15-21

THEN WENT the Pharisees, and took counsel how they might entangle him in his talk.

AND THEY sent out unto him their disciples with the Herodians, saying, Master, we know that thou art true, and teachest the way of God in truth, neither carest thou for any man: for thou regardest not the person of men.

TELL US therefore, What thinkest thou? Is it lawful to give tribute unto Caesar, or not?

BUT JESUS perceived their wickedness, and said, Why tempt ye me, ye hypocrites?

SHEW ME the tribute money. And they brought unto him a penny.

AND HE saith unto them, Whose is this image and superscription?

THEY SAY unto him, Caesar's. Then saith he unto them, Render therefore unto Caesar the things which are Caesar's; and unto God the things that are God's.

THE PHARISEES

The word 'pharisee' comes from the Hebrew word *perushim*, meaning separated. The *perushim* shunned all pagan influence, both cultural and religious, and also set themselves apart, through ritual purity, from all those in Israel who did not observe the Law.

The Pharisees emerged as a distinct religious party after the Maccabaean revolt (168–164 BC). Their attitude to the occupying powers was one of resignation: they were content to have achieved religious independence and knew that political freedom was impossible. Essentially realists, they withdrew their interest from Israel's political destiny and confined themselves to her religion.

For the Pharisees, as for all Jews, the Law was of supreme importance. Yet unlike other more rigid sects, they did not only adhere to the letter of the Torah, but updated it with an oral commentary. Their attitude was one of reverent argument carried out according to certain fixed rules. They added to the existing Law new laws based on the demands and needs of the day.

Several examples will show the effectiveness of the Oral Law. Firstly, divorce, which Moses had permitted, even making it relatively easy (Deut. 24:1). The Pharisees wanted to make it more difficult, in accordance with another biblical tradition that man and wife, once bound, could not be unbound (Gen. 1:27), but without going against Moses. This they did by making the sum of money to be settled on a divorced wife so high that it was very hard for a man to repudiate her. Secondly, Sabbath observance, a rigid biblical requirement: so many additional prohibitions had been derived from existing texts that it became impossible to do anything on the Sabbath—until the more liberal rabbis made exceptions when human, or even animal, life was at stake. Thirdly, the law that all debts must be cancelled in the seventh year, intended in Mosaic times to adjust the inequalities of fortune but the cause of much trouble in the more uncertain Herodian age, was modified

so that the creditor had the right to collect his outstanding debts before seven years. This was called the *prosbol*.

The teachings of the Pharisees came to be the orthodox Judaism of the day. They also believed in the resurrection of the dead, and looked forward to the Messianic age, although they did not emphasize the supernatural element of this idea. Essentially down-to-earth, they lived in the present where they sought to establish the Kingdom of God through obedience to the Law.

Like most religious groups, the Pharisees had a liberal and a conservative wing, led by the Rabbis Hillel and Shammai respectively. Hillel, who as a person was gentle, humane and saintly, was more lenient. He sought to encapsulate the Law in the maxim 'Do not unto others what you would not have others do to you', and in the ethics of love, justice and peace. Shammai on the other hand was much more rigorous in his application of the Law. The two men differed in method as well as in approach: Shammai refused to depart too far from the text of the Torah; Hillel developed an elaborate set of rules according to which it could be discussed.

The portrayal of the Pharisees in the Gospels is harsh, although a careful reading will show that some are mentioned as friends of Jesus. The accusations of hypocrisy too have their parallels in Jewish literature. Although there were some Pharisees who sought only to serve God and their neighbour, the basic weakness of others was legalism and adherence to tradition; Jesus by contrast responded to the needs of the invidual without legal barriers.

Ironically, it was the very clinging of the Pharisees to their idea of the Law which enabled Judaism to survive the birth of Christianity and the destruction of the Jewish state. When the Temple was burnt down and with it the scrolls of the Law, the Pharisees, who carried the Law in their hearts and not only on paper, continued their 'eternal discussion about the Eternal' and recorded it in the Talmud.

St Matthew
Chapter 23, verses 1-7; 23-26

THEN SPAKE Jesus to the multitude, and to his disciples,

SAYING, THE scribes and the Pharisees sit in Moses' seat:

ALL THEREFORE whatsoever they bid you observe, that observe and do; but do not ye after their works: for they say, and do not.

FOR THEY bind heavy burdens and grievous to be borne, and lay them on men's shoulders; but they themselves will not move them with one of their fingers.

BUT ALL their works they do for to be seen of men: they make broad their phylacteries, and enlarge the borders of their garments.

AND LOVE the uppermost rooms at feasts, and the chief seats in the synagogues,

AND GREETINGS in the markets, and to be called of men, Rabbi, Rabbi…

..WOE UNTO you, scribes and Pharisees, hypocrites! for ye pay tithe of mint and anise and cummin, and have omitted the weightier matters of the law, judgment, mercy, and faith: these ought ye to have done, and not to leave the other undone.

YE BLIND guides, which strain at a gnat, and swallow a camel.

WOE UNTO you, scribes and Pharisees, hypocrites! for ye make clean the outside of the cup and of the platter, but within they are full of extortion and excess.

THOU BLIND Pharisee, cleanse first that which is within the cup and platter, that the outside of them may be clean also.

St Luke
Chapter 22, verses 1-6

NOW THE feast of unleavened bread drew nigh, which is called the Passover.

AND THE chief priests and scribes sought how they might kill him; for they feared the people.

THEN ENTERED Satan into Judas surnamed Iscariot, being of the number of the twelve.

AND HE went his way, and communed with the chief priests and captains, how he might betray him unto them.

AND THEY were glad, and covenanted to give him money.

AND HE promised, and sought opportunity to betray him unto them in the absence of the multitude.

THE ZEALOTS

Some intensely nationalistic Jewish groups wanted to overthrow the Romans by force. Their nationalism was derived from their religious beliefs: for them as for all Jews God was the God of Israel and had revealed himself through the Law, part of whose function was to keep the Jew ritually separate from the heathen. This they took to its logical conclusion: they held that to have Israel occupied by an alien power, or even to have any contact with a pagan, was blasphemy. They looked for the immediate coming of the Messianic age: some believed that a political revolt against the alien forces would precipitate the advent of a heavenly Messiah; others expected an earthly, revolutionary leader who would overthrow the oppressor rather than meekly give himself up. Acknowledging no authority but that of God, and refuting that of man as represented by Caesar, they believed in the direct action of man to inaugurate God's kingdom.

There were two main nationalist groups: the Zealots and the Sicarii, an extreme manifestation of the Zealots. The Zealots consisted mainly of priests dedicated to keeping the Temple cult pure from any heathen influence, whose action in refusing any sacrifice from a non-Jew, and therefore from Caesar himself, helped spark off the final revolt. The Sicarii, by contrast, came from the ordinary people, and believed in guerilla warfare; they were a kind of social revolutionary group. Their name comes from the dagger (Latin *sica*) which they used not only in attacks against the Romans but also against those who collaborated with them.

The first significant uprising occurred in AD 6, in protest against the imperial tax ordered by Quirinus. It was led by Judas the Galilean. The revolt was crushed, and the freedom fighters who survived took to the deserts where they influenced innumerable revolts. They probably did not need to work hard to incite the passions of the Jewish people, who were bitterly frustrated and weighed down by the heavy burden of taxation.

The Roman oppression intensified under Pontius Pilate and succeeding procurators. Things came to a head in AD 66, when Eleazar, the Zealot leader, and Menachem, son of Judas and leader of the Sicarii, both appealed independently for a final struggle against the oppressor which would lead God to intervene in history. Conditions were now intolerable and the people rose to the challenge. The inevitable happened: the Jews for all their courage were no match for the military might of the Romans. In the terrible war that ensued tens of thousands of Jews were slaughtered, and eventually Jerusalem itself was razed to the ground.

The Zealots and the Sicarii made one last stand. When Jerusalem itself was lost, they retreated to Masada, the huge fortress built by Herod in the barren country close to the Dead Sea. When the fortress fell to the Romans, they chose mass suicide rather than be taken captive by the heathen and outlive the destruction of the Jewish state.

NOW BEFORE the feast of the passover, when Jesus knew that his hour was come that he should depart out of this world unto the Father, having loved his own which were in the world, he loved them unto the end.

AND SUPPER being ended, the devil having now put into the heart of Judas Iscariot, Simon's son, to betray him;

JESUS KNOWING that the Father had given all things into his hands, and that he was come from God, and went to God;

HE RISETH from supper, and laid aside his garments; and took a towel, and girded himself.

AFTER THAT he poureth water into a bason, and began to wash the disciples' feet, and to wipe them with the towel wherewith he was girded.

THEN COMETH he to Simon Peter: and Peter saith unto him, Lord, dost thou wash my feet?

JESUS ANSWERED and said unto him, What I do thou knowest not now; but thou shalt know hereafter.

PETER SAITH unto him, Thou shalt never wash my feet. Jesus answered him, If I wash thee not, thou has no part with me.

SIMON PETER saith unto him, Lord, not my feet only, but also my hands and my head.

So after he had washed their feet, and had taken his garments, and was set down again, he said unto them, Know ye what I have done to you?

Ye call me Master and Lord: and ye say well; for so I am.

If I then, your Lord and Master, have washed your feet; ye also ought to wash one another's feet.

For I have given you an example, that ye should do as I have done to you.

Take, eat: this is my body
St Mark
Chapter 14, verses 18-25

AND AS they sat and did eat, Jesus said, Verily I say unto you, One of you which eateth with me shall betray me.

AND THEY began to be sorrowful, and to say unto him one by one, Is it I? and another said, Is it I?

AND HE answered and said unto them, It is one of the twelve, that dippeth with me in the dish.

THE SON of man indeed goeth, as it is written of him: but woe to that man by whom the Son of man is betrayed! good were it for that man if he had never been born.

AND AS they did eat, Jesus took bread, and blessed, and brake it, and gave to them, and said, Take, eat: this is my body.

AND HE took the cup, and when he had given thanks, he gave it to them: and they all drank of it.

AND HE said unto them, This is my blood of the new testament, which is shed for many.

VERILY I say unto you, I will drink no more of the fruit of the vine, until that day that I drink it new in the kingdom of God.

St Matthew
Chapter 26, verses 36-45

THEN COMETH Jesus with them unto a place called Gethsemane, and saith unto the disciples, Sit ye here, while I go and pray yonder.

AND HE took with him Peter and the two sons of Zebedee, and began to be sorrowful and very heavy.

THEN SAITH he unto them, My soul is exceeding sorrowful, even unto death: tarry ye here, and watch with me.

AND HE went a little farther, and fell on his face, and prayed, saying, O my Father, if it be possible, let this cup pass from me: nevertheless not as I will, but as thou wilt.

AND HE cometh unto the disciples, and findeth them asleep, and saith unto Peter, What, could ye not watch with me one hour?

WATCH AND pray, that ye enter not into temptation; the spirit indeed is willing, but the flesh is weak.

HE WENT away again the second time, and prayed, saying, O my Father, if this cup may not pass away from me, except I drink it, thy will be done.

AND HE came and found them asleep again: for their eyes were heavy.

AND HE left them, and went away again, and prayed the third time, saying the same words.

THEN COMETH he to his disciples, and saith unto them, Sleep on now, and take your rest: behold, the hour is at hand, and the Son of man is betrayed into the hands of sinners.

AND IMMEDIATELY, while he yet spake, cometh Judas, one of the twelve, and with him a great multitude with swords and staves, from the chief priests and the scribes and the elders.

AND HE that betrayed him had given them a token, saying, Whomsoever I shall kiss, that same is he; take him, and lead him away safely.

AND AS soon as he was come, he goeth straightway to him and saith, Master, master; and kissed him.

AND THEY laid their hands on him, and took him.

AND ONE of them that stood by drew a sword, and smote a servant of the high priest, and cut off his ear.

AND JESUS answered and said unto them, Are ye come out, as against a thief, with swords and with staves to take me?

I WAS daily with you in the temple teaching, and ye took me not: but the scriptures must be fulfilled.

AND THEY all forsook him, and fled.

AND THERE followed him a certain young man, having a linen cloth cast about his naked body; and the young men laid hold on him:

AND HE left the linen cloth, and fled from them naked.

St Matthew
Chapter 26, verses 57-68

AND THEY that had laid hold on Jesus led him away to Caiaphas the high priest, where the scribes and the elders were assembled.

BUT PETER followed him afar off unto the high priest's palace, and went in, and sat with the servants, to see the end.

NOW THE chief priests, and elders, and all the council, sought false witness against Jesus, to put him to death;

BUT FOUND none: yea, though many false witnesses came, yet found they none. At the last came two false witnesses,

AND SAID, This fellow said, I am able to destroy the temple of God, and to build it in three days.

AND THE high priest arose, and said unto him, Answerest thou nothing? what is it which these witness against thee?

BUT JESUS held his peace. And the high priest answered and said unto him, I adjure thee by the living God, that thou tell us whether thou be the Christ, the Son of God.

JESUS SAITH unto him, Thou hast said: nevertheless I say unto you, Hereafter shall ye see the Son of man sitting on the right hand of power, and coming in the clouds of heaven.

THEN THE high priest rent his clothes, saying, He hath spoken blasphemy; what further need have we of witnesses? behold, now ye have heard his blasphemy.

WHAT THINK ye? They answered and said, He is guilty of death.

THEN DID they spit in his face, and buffeted him; and others smote him with the palms of their hands,

SAYING, PROPHESY unto us, thou Christ, Who is he that smote thee?

THE SADDUCEES

The word 'Sadducee' probably comes from the name 'Zadok', the High Priest of Solomon. Like other religious groups in the time of Jesus they became prominent in the second century BC, and may be described as the party of the establishment.

The Sadducees drew their members from the well-to-do, aristocratic classes, and it was not unusual for the High Priest himself to come from their ranks. Because of the political significance of this office in pre-Roman times, the Sadducees played an important role in the governing of the state as well as in religious affairs. When their power was curtailed by Herod along with that of the High Priest, they clung to their old ecclesiastical privileges and maintained an intense conservatism. They kept good relations with the Romans partly to further their own cause and partly because they genuinely believed that there was no other alternative for Israel but collaboration.

Their main point of disagreement with the Pharisees was over the Law. Whereas the latter had built up an oral tradition the Sadducees adhered strictly to the 613 precepts of the Written Law, and refused to elaborate on them. They also rejected many theological doctrines such as the resurrection of the dead or the survival of the soul, the existence of angels and of good and evil spirits, and the providential regulation of human affairs, on the grounds that none of these could be found in the existing canon of scriptures. Their political and religious conservatism thus counterbalance one another: sceptical of God's intervention in human affairs, and of man's ability to regulate the whole of life by the Torah, they rejected the idea of a theocratic state with a Jewish identity and clung to the *status quo*.

Because of their close connections with the chief priests the Sadducees had the upper hand in the Temple, conducting its ritual along their lines and administering justice from it according to a strict interpretation of the Torah. Because of their severity they were not much liked by the common people, and they were quick to stamp out anything that might smack of insurrection. After the destruction of Jerusalem in AD 70 they faded out as a religious party—a logical consequence of their inability to divorce the Torah, and with it the seat of spiritual power, from the Temple.

AND AS Peter was beneath in the palace, there cometh one of the maids of the high priest:

AND WHEN she saw Peter warming himself, she looked upon him, and said, And thou also wast with Jesus of Nazareth.

BUT HE denied, saying, I know not, neither understand I what thou sayest. And he went out into the porch; and the cock crew.

AND A maid saw him again, and began to say to them that stood by, This is one of them.

AND HE denied it again. And a little after, they that stood by said again to Peter, Surely thou art one of them: for thou art a Galilaean, and thy speech agreeth thereto.

BUT HE began to curse and to swear, saying, I know not this man of whom ye speak.

AND THE second time the cock crew. And Peter called to mind the word that Jesus said unto him, Before the cock crow twice, thou shalt deny me thrice. And when he thought thereon, he wept.

St John
Chapter 18, verses 28-40

THEN LED they Jesus from Caiaphas unto the hall of judgment: and it was early; and they themselves went not into the judgment hall, lest they should be defiled; but that they might eat the passover.

PILATE THEN went out unto them, and said, What accusation bring ye against this man?

THEY ANSWERED and said unto him, If he were not a malefactor, we would not have delivered him up unto thee.

THEN SAID Pilate unto them, Take ye him, and judge him according to your law. The Jews therefore said unto him, It is not lawful for us to put any man to death:

THAT THE saying of Jesus might be fulfilled, which he spake, signifying what death he should die.

THEN PILATE entered into the judgment hall again, and called Jesus, and said unto him, Art thou the King of the Jews?

JESUS ANSWERED him, Sayest thou this thing of thyself, or did others tell it thee of me?

PILATE ANSWERED, Am I a Jew? Thine own nation and the chief priests have delivered thee unto me: what hast thou done?

JESUS ANSWERED, My kingdom is not of this world: if my kingdom were of this world, then would my servants fight, that I should not be delivered to the Jews: but now is my kingdom not from hence.

PILATE THEREFORE said unto him, Art thou a king then? Jesus answered, Thou sayest that I am a king. To this end was I born, and for this cause came I into the world, that I should bear witness unto the truth. Every one that is of the truth heareth my voice.

PILATE SAITH unto him, What is truth? And when he had said this, he went out again unto the Jews, and saith unto them, I find in him no fault at all.

BUT YE have a custom, that I should release unto you one at the passover: will ye therefore that I release unto you the King of the Jews?

THEN CRIED they all again, saying, Not this man, but Barabbas. Now Barabbas was a robber.

St John

Chapter 19, verses 1-7

THEN PILATE therefore took Jesus, and scourged him.

AND THE soldiers platted a crown of thorns, and put it on his head, and they put on him a purple robe,

AND SAID, Hail, King of the Jews! And they smote him with their hands.

PILATE THEREFORE went forth again, and saith unto them, Behold, I bring him forth to you, that ye may know that I find no fault in him.

THEN CAME Jesus forth, wearing the crown of thorns, and the purple robe. And Pilate saith unto them, Behold the man!

WHEN THE chief priests therefore and officers saw him, they cried out, saying, Crucify him, crucify him. Pilate saith unto them, Take ye him, and crucify him: for I find no fault in him.

THE JEWS answered him, We have a law, and by our law he ought to die, because he made himself the Son of God.

WHEN PILATE therefore heard that saying, he was the more afraid,

AND WENT again into the judgment hall, and saith unto Jesus, Whence art thou? But Jesus gave him no answer.

THEN SAITH Pilate unto him, Speakest thou not unto me? knowest thou not that I have power to crucify thee, and have power to release thee?

JESUS ANSWERED, Thou couldest have no power at all against me, except it were given thee from above: therefore he that delivered me unto thee hath the greater sin.

AND FROM thenceforth Pilate sought to release him: but the Jews cried out, saying, If thou let this man go, thou art not Caesar's friend: whosoever maketh himself a king speaketh against Caesar.

WHEN PILATE therefore heard that saying, he brought Jesus forth, and sat down in the judgment seat in a place that is called the Pavement, but in the Hebrew, Gabbatha.

AND IT was the preparation of the passover, and about the sixth hour: and he saith unto the Jews, Behold your King!

BUT THEY cried out, Away with him, away with him, crucify him. Pilate saith unto them, Shall I crucify your King? The chief priests answered, We have no king but Caesar.

THEN DELIVERED he him therefore unto them to be crucified. And they took Jesus, and led him away.

St Luke
Chapter 23, verses 26-34

AND AS they led him away, they laid hold upon one Simon, a Cyrenian, coming out of the country, and on him they laid the cross, that he might bear it after Jesus.

AND THERE followed him a great company of people, and of women, which also bewailed and lamented him.

BUT JESUS turning unto them said, Daughters of Jerusalem, weep not for me, but weep for yourselves, and for your children.

FOR, BEHOLD, the days are coming, in the which they shall say, Blessed are the barren, and the wombs that never bare, and the paps which never gave suck.

THEN SHALL they begin to say to the mountains, Fall on us; and to the hills, Cover us.

FOR IF they do these things in a green tree, what shall be done in the dry?

AND THERE were also two other, malefactors, led with him to be put to death.

AND WHEN they were come to the place, which is called Calvary, there they crucified him, and the malefactors, one on the right hand, and the other on the left.

THEN SAID Jesus, Father, forgive them; for they know not what they do. And they parted his raiment, and cast lots.

St Luke
Chapter 23, verses 35-43

AND THE people stood beholding. And the rulers also with them derided him, saying, He saved others; let him save himself, if he be Christ, the chosen of God.

AND THE soldiers also mocked him, coming to him, and offering him vinegar,

AND SAYING, If thou be the king of the Jews, save thyself.

AND A superscription also was written over him in letters of Greek, and Latin, and Hebrew,
THIS IS THE KING OF THE JEWS.

AND ONE of the malefactors which were hanged railed on him, saying, If thou be Christ, save thyself and us.

BUT THE other answering rebuked him, saying, Dost not thou fear God, seeing thou art in the same condemnation?

AND WE indeed justly; for we receive the due reward of our deeds: but this man hath done nothing amiss.

AND HE said unto Jesus, Lord, remember me when thou comest into thy kingdom.

AND JESUS said unto him, Verily I say unto thee, To day shalt thou be with me in paradise.

St John
Chapter 19, verses 25-27

NOW THERE stood by the cross of Jesus his mother, and his mother's sister, Mary the wife of Cleophas, and Mary Magdalene.

WHEN JESUS therefore saw his mother, and the disciple standing by, whom he loved, he saith unto his mother, Woman, behold thy son!

THEN SAITH he to the disciple, Behold thy mother! And from that hour that disciple took her unto his own house.

THE DREAM OF THE ROOD

The Dream of the Rood

They drove dark nails through my side,
Open wounds of malice that abide
To be seen upon me. I durst not spurn
Our foes mocking us with hate and scorn.
I was wet with blood fallen from the man's breast
When soul went out, a wavering guest.
On that little hill I have overlived and borne
Cruel deeds. I saw stretched out and torn
Woeful, the Lord of Hosts.

Darkness has masked the failing day,
Our Healer's body, bloodless clay
Stretched on the gallows, the weak rain
Wraps round and hides. This world of pain
With all creation, cries its loss,
The fall of a king:
Christ is on the cross!
See, come from far, each man of good
Draws near the prince. And I, the Rood,
In sorrow, humbly to the sod
Bowed down. They took Almighty God
Out of hard pain. Limbweary lay
His corpse fallen on earth. But they
Stood at his head and beheld God
Who rested, lying spent after the great fight.
Before my sight—his slayer's sight—
They shaped his coffin of brightest stone.
They entombed the Lord
And in dusk, sorrowful,
Raised a mourning song.

They left me steamed with sweat,
With arrows hasped, with wounds o'erset:
We three stayed weeping
For his body, fair house of life grown cold.
We were hacked down—
Thrust in a pit. But his disciples found me,
His friends—On silver they wound me,
Wrapped me in gold.

From an Anglo-Saxon poem
Translated by Gavin Bone

JESUS DIES ON THE CROSS

Jesus dies on the cross

A few hours more,
A few minutes more,
A few instants more.
For thirty-three years it had been going on.
For thirty-three years you have lived fully minute after
   minute.
You can no longer escape, now; you are there, at the end
   of your life, at the end of your road.
You are at the last extremity, at the edge of a precipice.
You must take the last step,
The last step of love,
The last step of life that ends in death.

You hesitate.
Three hours are long, three hours of agony;
Longer than three years of life,
Longer than thirty years of life.

You must decide, Lord, all is ready around you.
You are there, motionless, on your Cross.
You have renounced all activity other than embracing
   these crossed planks for which you were made.
And yet, there is still life in your nailed body.
Let all mortal flesh die, and make way for eternity.

Now, life slips from each limb, one by one, finding refuge
   in his still beating heart.
Immeasurable heart,
Overflowing heart,
Heart heavy as the world, the world of sins and miseries
   that it bears.

Lord, one more effort.
Mankind is there, waiting unknowingly for the cry of its
   Saviour.
Your brothers are there; they need you.
Your Father bends over you, already holding out his arms.
Lord, save us,
Save us.

See.
He has taken his heavy heart,
And,
Slowly,
Laboriously,
Alone between heaven and earth,
In the awesome night,
With passionate love,
He has gathered his life,
He has gathered the sin of the world,
And in a cry,
He has given *all*.
'Father, into thy hands I commit my spirit.'

Christ has just died for us.

Lord, help me to die for you.
Help me to die for them.

From 'Prayers on the Way of the Cross', by Michel Quoist

137

St Matthew
Chapter 27, verses 45-46

NOW FROM the sixth hour there was darkness over all the land unto the ninth hour.

AND ABOUT the ninth hour Jesus cried with a loud voice, saying, Eli, Eli, lama sabachthani? That is to say, My God, my God, why hast thou forsaken me?

St John
Chapter 19, verses 28-30

AFTER THIS, Jesus knowing that all things were now accomplished, that the scripture might be fulfilled, saith, I thirst.

NOW THERE was set a vessel full of vinegar: and they filled a sponge with vinegar, and put it upon hyssop, and put it to his mouth.

WHEN JESUS therefore had received the vinegar, he said, It is finished.

St Luke
Chapter 23, verse 46

AND WHEN Jesus had cried with a loud voice, he said, Father, into thy hands I commend my spirit: and having said thus, he gave up the ghost.

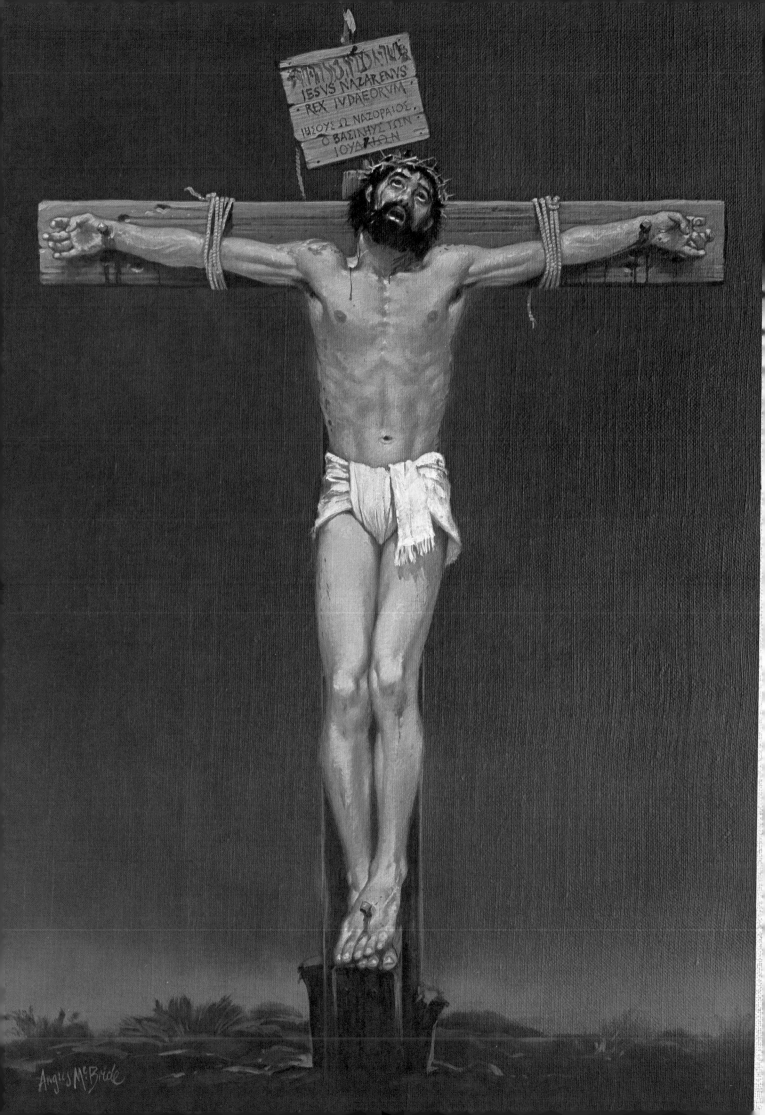

The rending of the temple veil
St Mark
Chapter 15, verses 38-39

AND THE veil of the temple was rent in twain from the top to the bottom.

Angus McBride

AND WHEN the centurion, which stood over against him, saw that he so cried out, and gave up the ghost, he said, Truly this man was the Son of God.

St Matthew
Chapter 27, verses 55-61

AND MANY women were there beholding afar off, which followed Jesus from Galilee, ministering unto him:

AMONG WHICH was Mary Magdalene, and Mary the mother of James and Joses, and the mother of Zebedee's children.

WHEN THE even was come, there came a rich man of Arimathaea, named Joseph, who also himself was Jesus' disciple:

HE WENT to Pilate, and begged the body of Jesus. Then Pilate commanded the body to be delivered.

AND WHEN Joseph had taken the body, he wrapped it in a clean linen cloth,

AND LAID it in his own new tomb, which he had hewn out in the rock: and he rolled a great stone to the door of the sepulchre, and departed.

AND THERE was Mary Magdalene, and the other Mary, sitting over against the sepulchre.

St John
Chapter 20, verses 1-10

THE FIRST day of the week cometh Mary Magdalene early, when it was yet dark, unto the sepulchre, and seeth the stone taken away from the sepulchre.

THEN SHE runneth, and cometh to Simon Peter, and to the other disciple, whom Jesus loved, and saith unto them, They have taken away the Lord out of the sepulchre, and we know not where they have laid him.

PETER THEREFORE went forth, and that other disciple, and came to the sepulchre.

SO THEY ran both together: and the other disciple did outrun Peter, and came first to the sepulchre.

AND HE stooping down, and looking in, saw the linen clothes lying; yet went he not in.

THEN COMETH Simon Peter following him, and went into the sepulchre, and seeth the linen clothes lie,

AND THE napkin, that was about his head, not lying with the linen clothes, but wrapped together in a place by itself.

THEN WENT in also that other disciple, which came first to the sepulchre, and he saw, and believed.

FOR AS yet they knew not the scripture, that he must rise again from the dead.

THEN THE disciples went away again unto their own home.

St John
Chapter 20, verses 11-18

BUT MARY stood without at the sepulchre weeping: and as she wept, she stooped down, and looked into the sepulchre,

AND SEETH two angels in white sitting, the one at the head, and the other at the feet, where the body of Jesus had lain.

AND THEY say unto her, Woman why weepest thou? She saith unto them, Because they have taken away my Lord, and I know not where they have laid him.

AND WHEN she had thus said, she turned herself back, and saw Jesus standing, and knew not that it was Jesus.

JESUS SAITH unto her, Woman, why weepest thou? whom seekest thou? She, supposing him to be the gardener, saith unto him, Sir, if thou have borne him hence, tell me where thou hast laid him, and I will take him away.

JESUS SAITH unto her, Mary. She turned herself, and saith unto him, Rabboni; which is to say, Master.

JESUS SAITH unto her, Touch me not; for I am not yet ascended to my Father: but go to my brethren, and say unto them, I ascend unto my Father, and your Father; and to my God, and your God.

MARY MAGDALENE came and told the disciples that she had seen the Lord, and that he had spoken these things unto her.

St Luke

Chapter 24, verses 13-35

AND, BEHOLD, two of them went that same day to a village called Emmaus, which was from Jerusalem about threescore furlongs

AND THEY talked together of all these things which had happened.

AND IT came to pass, that, while they communed together and reasoned, Jesus himself drew near, and went with them.

BUT THEIR eyes were holden that they should not know him.

AND HE said unto them, What manner of communications are these that ye have one to another, as ye walk, and are sad?

AND ONE of them, whose name was Cleopas, answering said unto him, Art thou only a stranger in Jerusalem, and hast not known the things which are come to pass there in these days?

AND HE said unto them, What things? And they said unto him, Concerning Jesus of Nazareth, which was a prophet mighty in deed and word before God and all the people:

AND HOW the chief priests and our rulers delivered him to be condemned to death, and have crucified him.

BUT WE trusted that it had been he which should have redeemed Israel: and beside all this, to day is the third day since these things were done.

YEA, AND certain women also of our company made us astonished, which were early at the sepulchre;

AND WHEN they found not his body, they came, saying, that they had also seen a vision of angels, which said that he was alive.

AND CERTAIN of them which were with us went to the sepulchre, and found it even so as the women had said: but him they saw not.

THEN HE said unto them, O fools, and slow of heart to believe all that the prophets have spoken:

OUGHT NOT Christ to have suffered these things, and to enter into his glory?

AND BEGINNING at Moses and all the prophets, he expounded unto them in all the scriptures the things concerning himself.

Except I shall see in his hands the print of the nails…
St John
Chapter 20, verses 19-20, 24-29

THEN THE same day at evening, being the first day of the week, when the doors were shut where the disciples were assembled for fear of the Jews, came Jesus and stood in the midst, and saith unto them, Peace be unto you.

AND WHEN he had so said, he shewed unto them his hands and his side. Then were the disciples glad, when they saw the Lord …

… BUT THOMAS, one of the twelve, called Didymus, was not with them when Jesus came.

THE OTHER disciples therefore said unto him, We have seen the Lord. But he said unto them, Except I shall see in his hands the print of the nails, and put my finger into the print of the nails, and thrust my hand into his side, I will not believe.

AND AFTER eight days again his disciples were within, and Thomas with them: then came Jesus, the doors being shut, and stood in the midst, and said, Peace be unto you.

THEN SAITH he to Thomas, Reach hither thy finger, and behold my hands; and reach hither thy hand, and thrust it into my side: and be not faithless, but believing.

AND THOMAS answered and said unto him, My Lord and my God.

JESUS SAITH unto him, Thomas, because thou hast seen me, thou hast believed: blessed are they that have not seen, and yet have believed.

St John
Chapter 21, verses 1-17

AFTER THESE things Jesus shewed himself again to the disciples at the sea of Tiberias; and on this wise shewed he himself.

THERE WERE together Simon Peter, and Thomas called Didymus, and Nathanael of Cana in Galilee, and the sons of Zebedee, and two other of his disciples.

SIMON PETER saith unto them, I go a fishing. They say unto him, We also go with thee. They went forth, and entered into a ship immediately; and that night they caught nothing.

BUT WHEN the morning was now come, Jesus stood on the shore: but the disciples knew not that it was Jesus.

THEN JESUS saith unto them, Children, have ye any meat? They answered him, No.

AND HE said unto them, Cast the net on the right side of the ship, and ye shall find. They cast therefore, and now they were not able to draw it for the multitude of fishes.

THEREFORE THAT disciple whom Jesus loved saith unto Peter, It is the Lord. Now when Simon Peter heard that it was the Lord, he girt his fisher's coat unto him, (for he was naked,) and did cast himself into the sea.

AND THE other disciples came in a little ship; (for they were not far from land, but as it were two hundred cubits,) dragging the net with fishes.

AS SOON then as they were come to land, they saw a fire of coals there, and fish laid thereon, and bread.

JESUS SAITH unto them, Bring of the fish which ye have now caught.

SIMON PETER went up, and drew the net to land full of great fishes, an hundred and fifty and three: and for all there were so many, yet was not the net broken.

JESUS SAITH unto them, Come and dine. And none of the disciples durst ask him, Who art thou? knowing that it was the Lord.

JESUS THEN cometh, and taketh bread, and giveth them, and fish likewise.

THIS IS now the third time that Jesus shewed himself to his disciples, after that he was risen from the dead.

SO WHEN they had dined, Jesus saith to Simon Peter, Simon, son of Jonas, lovest thou me more than these? He saith unto him, Yea, Lord; thou knowest that I love thee. He saith unto him, Feed my lambs.

HE SAITH to him again the second time, Simon, son of Jonas, lovest thou me? He saith unto him, Yea, Lord; thou knowest that I love thee. He saith unto him, Feed my sheep.

HE SAITH unto him the third time, Simon, son of Jonas, lovest thou me? Peter was grieved because he said unto him the third time, Lovest thou me? And he said unto him, Lord, thou knowest all things; thou knowest that I love thee. Jesus saith unto him, Feed my sheep.

St Matthew
Chapter 28, verses 16-20

THEN THE eleven disciples went away into Galilee, into a mountain where Jesus had appointed them.

AND WHEN they saw him, they worshipped him: but some doubted.

AND JESUS came and spake unto them, saying, All power is given unto me in heaven and in earth.

GO YE therefore, and teach all nations, baptizing them in the name of the Father, and of the Son, and of the Holy Ghost:

TEACHING THEM to observe all things whatsoever I have commanded you: and, lo, I am with you alway, even unto the end of the world. Amen.